A Survival Guide for
Hotel and Motel Professionals

Alan Gelb and Karen Levine

THOMSON

DELMAR LEARNING

Australia Canada Mexico Singapore Spain United Kingdom United States

THOMSON

DELMAR LEARNING

A Survival Guide for Hotel and Motel Professionals
Alan Gelb and Karen Levine

Vice President, Career Education Strategic Business Unit:
Dawn Gerrain

Director of Editorial:
Sherry Gomoll

Acquisitions Editor:
Matthew Hart

Editorial Assistant:
Lisa Flatley

Director of Production:
Wendy A. Troeger

Production Manager:
Carolyn Miller

Production Editor:
Kathryn B. Kucharek

Director of Marketing:
Wendy Mapstone

Cover Design:
Joe Villanova

For permission to use material from this text or product, submit a request online at http://www.thomsonrights.com Any additional questions about permissions can be submitted by email to thomsonrights@thomson.com

Library of Congress Cataloging-in-Publication Data

Gelb, Alan.
  A survival guide for hotel and motel professionals / by Alan Gelb & Karen Levine.
    p. cm.
  Includes index.
  ISBN 1-4018-4094-9
  1. Hotel management. I. Levine, Karen. II. Title.

TX911.3.M27G445 2004
647.94'068—dc22   2004055301

NOTICE TO THE READER

Contents

Acknowledgments

We would like to thank the many professionals who took the time to share their thoughts, insights, and reflections. We would particularly like to thank Anthony J. (Toby) Strianese, Chairperson of Hotel, Culinary Arts and Tourism Department, Schenectady County Community College, for all of his expertise and advice. We would also like to thank Lisa Flatley of Thomson Delmar Learning for her help.

Chapter 1

How Was Your Stay?

*W*hen interviewing people for this book, we discovered that quite a few had decided, at an early age, that the hotel and motel industry was where they had the best chance of finding the job of their dreams. Why? There were many reasons. Some remembered fun family vacations to resorts when they were little, and they wanted that fun to continue. After all, a career in the hotel and motel industry offers travel and luxury and the opportunity to meet people from all over the world. Many of those with whom we spoke had held summer jobs or part-time jobs at hotels or motor lodges, and they enjoyed the lively atmosphere and interaction with guests. And then there were a few who, as youngsters, had read the children's classic *Eloise*, about the little girl who grows up in the Plaza Hotel in New York City, and they couldn't imagine anything better than that. To spend one's life in and around a great hotel is a wonderful fantasy. The point is, many people who work in this industry love what they do and wouldn't dream of being in any other field. How about you? How did you become interested?

Before we go any farther, let's define our terms. When we speak about the hotel and motel field, we're referring to one arm of the much larger hospitality industry. The idea of "hospitality"—the culture and practice of taking care of travelers—emerged from the ancient tradition of trade. Think back to the days of Marco Polo, when silk and spice traders and such were crisscrossing the globe. Those folks buying and selling wares needed a place to eat and sleep, so this concept of hospitality came into play.

In fact, the first overnight lodgings date back over 4,000 years and were designed to accommodate travelers on Middle Eastern caravan routes. These lodgings, known as "caravanserai," were primitive structures, situated at eight-mile intervals, providing shelter to travelers and their animals. All of the necessary provisions—food, water, and bedding—were brought along by the guests. By the time of the Roman Empire, however, lodgings had become quite elaborate, and guests at hotels on the many roads that led to Rome could expect to find a restaurant, a lavatory, rooms with keys, and other such amenities.

The rise in religion also sparked a new desire to travel. Consider the great pilgrimages, for instance, with millions of worshippers taking to the road on spiritual journeys. These people had to be housed and fed. Monasteries and priories—safe, clean havens—vied with inns and taverns of often shockingly low repute to give these pilgrims a night's sleep in a warm bed or, failing that, on a straw pallet.

The idea of travel, geared for educational and cultural growth, emerged during the Renaissance. "The Grand Tour" was particularly popular among British scholars, and it involved trips to places such as Florence, Rome, Paris, Venice, Vienna, and Munich to study the arts and sciences. Lavish resorts and spas were established to meet the needs of these often well-heeled sightseers.

As shipping and rail technology developed, the world grew more and more interconnected, and hospitality needs greatly increased. The twentieth century saw the advent of the automobile and the airplane, both of which ushered in even more changes in the hospitality industry. Most parts of the world were now accessible, and an explosion of cultural exchange followed. The hotel and motel industry boomed.

It's important to understand that the hotel and motel industry is a part of the larger travel and tourism industry. Many hotels, lodges, and inns are entities of corporations that also own travel agencies, rental car outfits, bus lines, and so forth. Think of these intertwined industries as a kind of vast network that essentially has five distinct areas. One area addresses the issues and needs around *transportation*—airlines, railroads, the maritime industry, and so on. Another area concerns itself specifically with *travel and tourism*— travel agencies, Internet travel services, tours, and more. Moving along to the area of *recreation, sports, and entertainment*, you'll find the theme parks, national parks, stadiums, museums, tourist attractions, and such that people visit when they travel. Next is a very important area for travelers, the *food service* sector, which includes restaurants, bars, clubs, catering and banquet operations, and more. Finally we come to the area of the hospitality industry that we will be examining in this book, *lodging*, which includes hotels, motels, and resorts. And this is where you'll be checking in . . .

You should know, right from the start, that you've selected quite a career for yourself. Hotels, motels, inns, resorts, spas, lodges, bed-and-breakfasts— together they employ millions of people and generate revenues in the tens of billions of dollars. According to an article in *Hotel and Motel Management* (October 6, 2003), which cited recent numbers from the U.S. Bureau of Labor Statistics, over 1.8 million people are employed in this industry, and annual revenues exceed $80 billion. Even in the wake of September 11, 2001, with the outbreak of organized terrorism throughout the world—probably the most difficult period in the history of the lodging industry—people are still traveling. The increasing globalism of business *demands* that people travel. So don't pay too much attention to the gloom-and-doom forecasts. The lodging industry is not going to go away.

The field you've selected also happens to be absolutely fascinating. Just think about the personal talents and abilities it calls for. People working in the upper reaches of this field need to have a good grasp of a range of disciplines, including economics, marketing, real estate, law, data processing, psychology, and more. If you fantasize about life at the top—as a general manager of a large hotel, let's say—you should know that the individuals who hold these positions tend to share certain traits and characteristics. For example, most aren't afraid to work hard. A GM (general manager) should expect to rise early in the day and finish work late at night.

There is a great deal of pressure in this field, and your ability to withstand that pressure will be key to your success. With the long and late hours, all that time on your feet, and the difficulties in dealing with the needs of your staff and guests, you may feel as though the tension is more than you can bear at times. Effective ways to handle stress are covered in this book, particularly in the area of time management, so often one of the chief culprits in creating unnecessary pressure.

Professionals in the hotel and motel industry also should possess good communication skills. On any given day, a GM will field dozens, if not hundreds, of phone calls and e-mails. This book provides helpful hints about effective communication—how to speak and write clearly so your words will be understood. People in management positions in this field also should be reasonably confident. Often they will be asked to make on-the-spot decisions to try to resolve all of the problems, big and small, that arise on a daily basis. We discuss issues of self-esteem and goal setting that may impact on one's confidence.

Anyone who is a manager in the hotel and motel industry will tell you that one of the most important predictors of success in one's job is whether or not one has a knack for teamwork. Each individual who works in a hotel or motel scenario is important. The person who makes the beds, carries the bags, fixes the pipes, books the rooms, audits the books, hires the staff, oversees security . . . each of these individuals is vital to the ongoing success of the establishment. One of the chapters in this book is dedicated to the principle of teamwork, and it is filled with important tips on how to function as a member of a team.

Organizational skills are important in this industry. You have to learn how to stay on top of your papers, your phone calls, and, as we said earlier, your time. But even if you worry that you're a bit scattered, be assured that anyone can learn to become better organized. We'll tell you all about prioritizing, motivating yourself, and avoiding the traps of procrastination and perfectionism.

If you sometimes forget that you're in a service industry, your guests won't, particularly if they're not very pleased with your service. Remember that most travelers feel vulnerable, to a certain extent, and that savvy travelers expect good value for their money. We will explore the crucial ways in which you can convey to your guests just how important they are. If you learn your lessons well, perhaps you'll be rewarded with repeat visits from them.

We also want to stress that as a player in the hotel and motel industry, you can expect to find yourself in a position where other people's safety, if not their lives, depends on you. It is vitally important to educate yourself about the basic issues of safety and sanitation as they apply to your work. We offer valuable information in this regard.

Of course, you'll want to know how to find a job in this field and how to advance from one position to another. Our concluding chapter provides excellent tips on important aspects of the job search, from résumé writing to interviewing to salary negotiations and more.

The tips and insights we've gathered from your colleagues working in the hotel and motel industry hopefully will inspire you to make valuable changes in the way you do things and alert you to the pitfalls you need to avoid. We begin our discussion by hearing some of the responses from our professionals to the question: "What's the first thing people should know when they decide to enter this field?"

👑 It's one of the biggest clichés in the book, but like most clichés, it's grounded in truth: the customer is always right. That doesn't mean that the customer is *literally* always right, but it means that your attitude toward the customer is that he or she is the person who needs to be comforted and taken care of and made to feel that he or she is the most important person in the room. That's the essence of a service profession, and until you internalize this attitude, so that you don't even have to *think* about it, you're not really going to be able to perform at your best in this field.

👑 When you work in the hotel and motel industry, you have to realize that you're dealing with people *in need*. They're tired—maybe they've been on a plane for hours. They're hungry. They're in a strange part of the world where they don't speak the language. Maybe they're in for a wedding or some other big event, and emotions are running high. If they're on business travel, they have a whole other set of needs. As someone who works in the hotel and motel industry, you have to recognize that you've made an ethical commitment to helping these people feel more comfortable and secure. You have to do everything you can to make their visit a good one and to alleviate their stress, not add to it.

👑 What I love about this business is the constant influx of interesting stimuli. I'm always meeting people from all over the world. I hear different languages. I see different styles of dress, and I witness different ways of interacting. Sometimes that's a challenge, but it doesn't have to be an unpleasant challenge. To me, it all becomes an opportunity to learn. I'd have to say that working in the hotel and motel industry is like being on a constant learning curve, and the upside of that is that you're never bored!

👑 I started out working in a big motel chain, outside of El Paso, Texas. Today, I'm the manager of housekeeping services for a luxury hotel in Bermuda. Am I the "Great American Success Story"? Hardly. I'm just a gal who's worked hard, who's always taken on more, who feels a responsibility about what I do, and that's how I've moved ahead in this business. And believe me, I'm not one of a kind. There are a lot of people like me out there who have done very well in this field.

♕ Let's call a spade a spade: it's not an easy business. Not for the faint of heart. Since 1995, I've managed a small luxury hotel in San Francisco, and believe me, if you think it's easy to stay afloat when everybody and their brother is finding bargains on the Internet and is staying at the big chains—well, it's not so easy. And the climate after September 11 has made everything twice as hard. Not only are people traveling less, but you have all these new security issues to deal with. Sometimes I think to myself, why didn't I become a high school biology teacher like my brother did? You have regular hours. You go home at night to eat dinner with your family. You have the summers off. After a few years, they give you tenure, and from then on, you have unbelievable job security. But hey—I *didn't* become a high school teacher. I became a hotel manager. And the weird thing is that I love it. I roam the halls and the kitchen and the rooms of this old place, and it's my second home. Really. In some ways it's even more of a home to me than my apartment is. Do I have a life? You bet I do. A crazy life sometimes, but I wouldn't trade it for anything.

♕ When I was a kid, back in the '80s, I used to watch the TV series *Hotel* every week. Anyway, almost from the beginning, that show got me fascinated with the whole world of hotels, and when I went to school, I decided to study hotel administration. I've worked in Denver, L.A., Philadelphia, and now I'm in New York City. And you know what? My life actually is a little bit like that show. I mean, hotels really *are* pretty exciting, dramatic places. In one room, you could have a foreign diplomat; in another, an actress with her publicist, giving interviews for her new movie; in a third, you might have some couple from Kankakee, here in Manhattan to celebrate their 50th wedding anniversary; in another room, there's a mom and her sick child on a Make-A-Wish [Foundation] trip. I mean, when you come down to it, there's just a lot of built-in drama in the hotel world, and that's why I love it.

First and foremost—you have to know what you're doing. You're handling some really big-time responsibilities when you work in the hotel business. There can be fires and assaults and thefts and rapes and . . . well, you get the idea. I think it's absolutely critical to have an awareness of all that and to assume equal responsibility with a real seriousness of purpose.

It's important to understand that there is *a lot* of pressure in this business, and the higher up you go, the more pressure you'll find. And why all the pressure? Because you've got to sell rooms. That's the bottom line, folks. In this business, you've got something to sell—hotel space, whether guest rooms or function rooms or whatever—and, as with any selling business, until you make your sales, there's considerable pressure. Go into any real estate office or any car dealership and you'll see exactly what I'm talking about. Go into any hotel, and if the phones haven't been ringing and rooms aren't being booked, it's not going to be a happy place.

I enjoy this field because I think of myself as a person who strives for excellence, on a personal level anyway, and in the hotel field, I can work toward excellence on an institutional level. I actually think that excellence is something that we, as human beings, can all strive for in almost any situation, but in the hotel field, excellence—or the lack of it—is so tangible. I love to be surrounded by well-kept appointments, vacuumed rugs, fresh flowers, gleaming, silver-plated trays that have scrumptious dishes on them being delivered by room service personnel wearing pristine white jackets. Call me a clean freak, but I find that having those kinds of goals and being able to realize those goals is a great source of satisfaction.

👑 It's important to know right at the start that working in this field may involve your making very real sacrifices on the quality-of-life front. Hotels are open on Christmas and New Year's Eve and Thanks-giving, and more than likely you're going to be work-ing at least some of those days. Your brother-in-law, the letter carrier, may get to sit around your house drinking eggnog on Christmas day and playing with your kid's new electric railroad, but you can't go crazy because *you've* got to go to work. That's the deal.

👑 You have to be realistic about this field. When you go into it, maybe you're dreaming of the Waldorf and having kings and queens as your guests. When you enter the real world, you may very well find yourself working in a motor lodge in Kansas City, and the only kings and queens you'll be seeing are on a deck of cards. But that's okay. What you come to understand is that it's not so much the glamour that's the driving force in your professional life but the sense of professionalism you bring to your work. Doing the best job you can do wherever you are can feel really good. I get a lot of satisfaction out of the fact that I've made our operation function more smoothly than the guy who came before me.

 What's the first thing I'd tell anyone entering this field? That's easy—that there's endless opportunity. There really is. If you're willing to work hard, and if you have the attitude that your learning never stops, then you can keep on climbing the ladder in this business. There's truly no ceiling as to what you can achieve. Keep in mind that there's a real entre-preneurial bent running through this field. Today, you might be a bell captain. Tomorrow, you could own a bed and breakfast. Somewhere in your future, there might be a hotel. No kidding. Anything's possible.

The Cast of Characters

The hotel and motel industry offers many interesting career opportunities. The particular job you wind up in will have a lot to do with your particular set of skills and interests. Are you good with figures? Are you a real "people person"? Is food and drink your first love? Do you enjoy the challenge of sales? Do you have your finger on the pulse of the city? Are you a generalist who's good at many things? Let's take a look at each position we'll be examining in this book to see which one sounds good to you.

The Food and Drink People

The food and drink people are the folks who take care of hungry and thirsty guests.

Food and Beverage Director Also known as the food and beverage manager, or controller, this individual supervises the operation of the coffee shop, dining room, lounge, and banquet facilities. In this position of great responsibility, the director will hire and train staff, deal with finances and accounting, oversee all purchases and requisitions for the kitchen and dining room, interface with customers to make sure they are satisfied, and more.

Banquet and Catering Manager The banquet and catering manager is responsible for the daily operation of a banquet facility. Like the food and beverage director, this individual directly supervises employees and hires and trains staff. He or she also is in charge of scheduling and may assist in food preparation and plating food, as necessary. Interfacing with guests to answer any inquiries or resolve any complaints is another aspect of the job.

Catering Sales Manager Also known as the banquet sales manager, this individual books the meeting, banquet, and group rooms. He or she coordinates schedules with meeting and banquet planners to confirm details related to the function, works with customers to discuss details, and ensures the smooth execution of events.

For tips that relate to other workers in the food and beverage area—including those that relate to maître d's, waitstaff, bartenders, and such—consult our book *A Survival Guide for Restaurant Professionals* (Thomson Delmar Learning, 2004).

Guest Contact Staff

If you're a "people person," you might enjoy being a member of the guest contact staff. Positions include the following:

Doorperson Though not always the first person to greet a guest (that honor may fall to the parking valet, whose job we will not cover in this book), the doorperson is found in better hotels. He or she helps with the transition of the arriving (or departing) vehicle and the lobby area. Traditionally the doorperson helped guests secure cabs. Today, in smaller hotels, this position has either been phased out or is incorporated into the bell staff.

Bellperson Today when we speak about this vital cog in the hotel and motel industry, we no longer use the words "bellman," "bellhop," or "bellboy." The bellperson escorts the guest to his or her room . . . "rooming the guest" is the industry phrase. In addition to rooming guests, the bellperson assists in other departments as needed, such as with parking, housekeeping, and restaurant duties. Bellpersons also deliver flowers, fruit baskets, messages, and faxes to guests' rooms. Even in this era of political correctness, the chief bellperson is still known as the "bell captain."

Front Desk Staff The front desk staff is comprised of the front office manager, the front desk supervisor, and the front desk agents or clerks. Their tasks include: guest check-in and registration; the selection and assignment of guest rooms; establishing credit and determining method of payment; opening, posting, and closing guest accounts; cashing personal checks and traveler's checks and exchanging foreign currency; handling guest complaints; and completing guest checkouts.

Rooms Controller The rooms controller "blocks" the rooms. "Blocking a room" means matching guests' room preferences to available rooms.

Concierge The concierge is the "point person" who takes care of many odds and ends for guests. He or she might, for instance, secure tickets for theater or sporting events, book reservations for airlines, car rentals, and restaurants, or offer advice regarding local attractions, including driving directions and information about shops, restaurants, and cultural activities.

Reservationist The reservationist takes the reservations, usually over the phone. This individual must be knowledgeable, thorough, courteous, and able to solve problems.

The "Number Cruncher"

If you're good with figures, maybe you'll wind up a "number cruncher." Jobs that fall under this category include:

Controller The hotel controller is in charge of all financial reporting and cash flow management and is responsible for monitoring costs and determining cash expenditures.

Accounting Staff Members of the accounting staff monitor and manage the money. This department handles credit, accounts receivable, accounts payable, and the night audit.

Night Auditor The night audit might be assigned to an employee called, logically, the "night auditor." Duties include balancing the daily audit figures, along with some housekeeping assignments, customer service, setting up the continental breakfast in certain establishments, checking guests in and out, selling rooms to walk-ins, and taking reservations.

Supervisory and Support Staff

The supervisory and support staff will handle just about everything that we have not previously covered. Jobs in this area include the following:

Marketing Members of the marketing department, headed by the director of marketing, oversee the hotel's sales and marketing operations, ensuring that the hotel maximizes its room revenues.

Maintenance The maintenance department, headed by the chief engineer, oversees all operations regarding the maintenance and security of the establishment. The director of grounds is in charge of the maintenance of all outdoor space. The executive housekeeper heads the housekeeping aspect of this area and reports to the director of services, who can be viewed as the "behind-the-scenes" equivalent of the front officer manager.

 **Human Resources** Led by the director of human resources, the human resources department attends to the hiring and firing of employees.

 **Recreation** The recreation department is led by the director of recreation, who supervises the golf pro, the tennis pro, the manager of aquatics, the spa manager, and the children's activity manager, if the operation encompasses such functions.

Last, but hardly least, is the general manager, who is assisted by the director of operations. Many other jobs can be found in this field—far more than we could possibly cover here. Right now, however, we'd like to move on to the Seven Guiding Principles, life changers from which anyone in any of these jobs can benefit.

The Seven Guiding Principles

Once you've read through the Seven Guiding Principles, you'll want to do your best to keep them firmly in your mind. The way you choose to do so is up to you. You may find it best to write them out and keep them in a card in your wallet, to be pulled out during quiet moments. Or perhaps you might find it useful to tape the card onto the dashboard of your car and review these principles when you're stopped at a traffic light. If you're more of an auditory learner than a visual one, you might make a tape in which you state the principles, then listen to the tape as you drive or work out. Perhaps your best bet would be to turn these principles into some kind of rhyme or counting song that you can chant whenever you get the chance—when you rise or before you go to sleep.

Your goal in internalizing the Seven Guiding Principles is to develop a healthy, "holistic" perspective about your career that can sustain you over the long run. Success may be a great thing, but let's not forget that the healthiest goal is to enjoy life, have fun doing what you're doing, and be able to remember, at the end of the day, what you love most about your work and why you chose to go into this field.

Principle #1: Become an Active Listener

In some fields, people work pretty much on their own, but this is not true of the hotel and motel industry. Here you're part of a team, no matter what level you find yourself on. If you've had any experience being on a team, then you know how vital it is to be able to listen and hear what your teammates are trying to tell you. If you're in a huddle on a football field and you can't hear your teammates, then you might go one way when everybody else is going the other!

Your success in this field is linked to your ability to communicate. Once you assume any kind of managerial duties, your need to communicate becomes doubly important. You have to motivate people, and in order to motivate them, they have to believe that you can hear them. If they sense otherwise, they may wind up feeling neglected, ignored, angry, and disappointed with you. Their negative feelings can easily translate into negative job performance, which in turn will reflect negatively on you.

The key to communication is good listening. The better we become at listening—the more we train ourselves to *hear* what is said—the more we can expect to get out of our work life and out of life in general.

Later in this book, we'll discuss the importance of good listening skills, with specific techniques. For now, however, let's begin with the first of our Seven Guiding Principles—*become an active listener*. Take time out of your busy day to listen to others and to really hear what they have to say. Living in this noisy, modern world of ours can make it easy to block things out. Some of us travel to and from work with headphones on. Too many of us are slaves to our cell phones. We are all so inundated with the babble of modern technology that we have to "filter out" a variety of stimuli. This "filtering-out" process may seem like self-preservation, but over time it can actually intensify your experience of stress. You may begin to feel isolated, as though there's an invisible wall separating you from others. In fact, by the end of this book, you may realize that you can better handle stress by keeping the lines of communication open. If you manage to do this, chances are you'll benefit from the contact and camaraderie with your colleagues and customers. Keep in mind, however, that when we talk about communication, we're talking about engaging with others in *real* dialogue. Real dialogue is saying what you have to say and listening to what others say to you.

Principle #2: Think Outside of the Box

In considering Principle #2, let us first define our terms. What exactly do we mean by "the box"? We are referring to that place you put yourself into, day in and day out. For some, that place may feel comfortable; for others, it may feel tight and restrictive. But any way you look at it, it's still a box, and you're still limiting yourself by remaining within its four walls.

Maybe you're viewing the box as the hotel you've been working for. When you began this career, you imagined yourself on the Big Island of Hawaii, in a resort where palm trees grew in an atrium, where guests lounged on recliners, sipping rum drinks out of pineapples, and where the sunsets painted unforgettable pictures every night of the week. Now you wake up and you're working at the front desk of a hotel in New Haven, Connecticut, which is several stars away from four, where the winters are long and gray, and where the only pineapple in sight comes out of a can. Well, friends, that's reality. But that reality doesn't have to be a box. The box is simply of your own making, and there are all kinds of ways out of it. Taking up a new interest—swimming let's say, or bird-watching— is a great way to break out of the box. Going on a vacation—to New Orleans for jazz or to Montreal for French food—can be marvelous therapy. Or maybe you'll want to get together once a month with friends to eat out at a new restaurant. The goal is to get some *new* ideas. Keep in mind, too, that continuing education is a reliable prescription for living by our second guiding principle. As long as you're learning, it's quite likely that you'll be thinking outside of that box.

Principle #3: Take Time to Figure Out What You Find Most Satisfying

Some lucky people start out in life quite clear about what they love and what they want to do for a living. They enjoy exercise, so they become fitness trainers. They love to use building blocks, so they become civil engineers. They enjoy cutting out paper dolls, so they become fashion designers. But not everyone can identify their first love and what they want to do with their lives. For many of us, it's a hit-or-miss process.

We think we're going to become musicians, but lo and behold, we realize that there are many great musicians who are more talented and dedicated than we are. We think we're going to become physicians, but life intrudes, and the sacrifice we'd have to make for our studies doesn't seem viable. As we said at the beginning of this chapter, many of the people we interviewed for this book fell in love with the idea of working in this industry early in their lives because of their positive experiences at hotels and resorts. Others in the field may have entered "through the back door." Perhaps you knew someone who recommended you for a job when you needed it. Or maybe your mother or father worked in the field and persuaded you to give it a try. In introducing the third principle, we urge you to find something in your life that you feel passionate about and that satisfies your longings, because this awareness can truly change your life.

In developing our Seven Guiding Principles, we discovered the work of Mihaly Cziksentmihalyi, Ph.D., professor of psychology at the Drucker School of Management at Clermont Graduate University. In a groundbreaking study that he conducted with a group of adolescents, Cziksentmihalyi produced findings we felt were relevant to our discussion. The adolescents in his study were outfitted with beepers that went off eight times a day over a one-week period each year. Every time the beepers signaled, the adolescents would report to Cziksentmihalyi about what they were doing and how they were feeling about the activity. Among other things, Cziksentmihalyi found that when his subjects were involved in activities they enjoyed, they were able to develop a sense of what he called "flow," that great feeling of energy that makes people want to continue what they're doing and return to it whenever possible.

In our next chapter, we offer a tool and a technique to help you decide which activities give you the greatest sense of flow. You'll learn how to keep track of the way you spend your time, and you'll be able to assess how you really feel about what you're doing. We'll take you through your day in detail—before, after, and during work—and we'll show you how to make a meaningful analysis that will point to those activities that leave you feeling the most and the least satisfied. This honest assessment is a critical step before moving on to Principle #4.

Principle #4: Create Time for the Things You Care About

As a professional in the hotel and motel industry, you may find yourself working long and irregular hours. Chances are, you're also overtired. After all, irregular hours impact on one's sleep. This is the time to "recharge." Recharging requires you to be proactive and to make significant changes in your life. Maybe you'll want to spend more time with less people, substituting real intimacy for "business socializing." Or perhaps you'll need to find an hour in the day when you can attend to your physical well-being—working out, swimming, or practicing yoga or meditation. If you're looking to make some changes in your life and you live with someone, then perhaps it will make sense for you and your partner to exchange jobs and chores. Can your partner water the plants or walk the dogs while you do what you need to do for yourself? You can then make up for it on the other end of the day, perhaps cooking dinner while your partner goes for a brisk walk.

Now don't shake your head and say "impossible." Anything's possible, and too many of us carry around a "can't-do" attitude, when the fact is, we "*can* do." We *can* make changes in our lives, even if they're small, subtle ones. In time, even those small, subtle changes can have a powerful effect. The point is, you really owe it to yourself to make the effort, because when you start to meet your own needs, you stand a better chance of meeting the needs of others.

Principle #5: *Learn to Enjoy What's in Front of You*

If you've ever spent time exploring aspects of the world's religions, you may have come across one of the core ideas of Buddhism, the principle of "mindfulness." What does it mean to live a "mindful" existence? It means living *in the moment*, not looking back with regret or ahead with anxiety.

Learning to live in the moment is a lot harder than it sounds, but it's also enormously beneficial to those attempting to clear away the clutter in their lives. As a busy professional in the hotel and motel industry, you may often feel that you have too much on your plate. Maybe you're supervising a team of individuals and each member has been coming to you lately with a particular set of complaints. Maybe you're dealing with contractors who are hard to work with. Is your boss difficult? Do your guests seem harder to please than usual? All or any of the above can present massive distractions in your life, causing you to always be in *another* place rather than the place you occupy in real space and time.

Think about it. Do you find yourself driving along on a beautiful day, worrying about the new person you've hired who's already been late twice this month, or remembering the unpleasant encounter you had yesterday with a guest who said her ring had been stolen . . . until she found it in her shoe? Does this kind of static prevent you from enjoying the glorious sunset or the amazing jazz combo on the radio?

Allowing yourself to live "mindfully"—to simply note and experience and enjoy what is going on in the here and now rather than obsessing about what could have been or might be—is a truly revolutionary way to live. Indeed, no matter how much you actually enjoy your work and appreciate the life you've made for yourself, it's difficult to resist the pull of your daily routines. Sometimes it's nearly impossible to ignore the petty disappointments and frustrations encountered each day. The practice of mindfulness provides an extraordinary means by which to massage ourselves "back into shape." Making a bed doesn't have to be a bore. It could be a time for you to appreciate the clean, crisp linens or the competence that you bring to your task. Receiving a produce shipment does not just have to be "work." It also could be a time when you delight in the beauty of a box full of ripe pears. Developing a mindful openness to the real sensual pleasures around you can help enormously to restore your appetite for your life and for your work.

Principle #6: Learn to Be Flexible

What's a day without a crisis? Certainly nothing you've ever encountered, we'd wager. In the hotel and motel business, plenty of unexpected events can throw your day out of whack. How about a blackout or brownout? A case of food poisoning? A theft? Rowdy, drunken guests who have trashed a room? How you respond when things go awry will say a lot about your ability to sustain yourself in this industry over the long run. Are you the sort to pull out your hair, gnash your teeth, or scream at your underlings? Do you punish yourself instead of others, suffering from migraines, acid reflux, or a variety of other ills? If your answer to either of these questions is yes, then now is an excellent time to take stock of your life and make changes.

Imagine that you're a highly disciplined person who always does what you set out to do. You're more than willing to work the longest hours, expend the most energy, and kick into overdrive when crises hit and the going gets tough. You like to think of yourself as a well-honed machine that can get the job done. Well, that may be a reasonable model for your professional conduct, if you so choose, but don't get too carried away with the metaphor. After all, you wouldn't want to drive a machine into the ground, would you? Machines need to be taken care of. You have to clean a machine, replace any broken parts, and keep it lubricated so its gears won't grind against each other and wear down. If you enjoy thinking of yourself as a machine—a super-sophisticated machine that can do anything asked of it—then we urge you to think of flexibility as the lubricant that will preserve your working parts. Flexibility is your best weapon against stress, as it may soften the sharp edges that often can factor into your interactions with others. If you sometimes feel like a rubber band ready to snap or a frayed, old piece of elastic that can no longer hold up its end, then flexibility is what will keep the rubber supple and the elastic firm and pliable. Like mindfulness, flexibility is a resource that is totally available to you, and it can be developed and strengthened the more you practice it.

Principle #7: Prioritize

Last, but certainly not least, is our seventh principle: to prioritize. Hopefully our other principles will help you focus on what you like to do and how you can best handle the things you may not particularly enjoy. Principle #7 can help you begin to sharpen those skills of differentiation. If you learn to prioritize, then you'll be able to arrange things so that the tasks that drag you down can be minimized and the ones that boost your feelings of well-being can be maximized. When you start keeping track of your time, which we will show you how to do in the next chapter, it can come as a great surprise to see how much actual choice you have in deciding where to devote your energies. Begin prioritizing by asking yourself key questions such as the following:

🔱 *In order to take care of myself, what do I need to do that no one else can do for me?* Maybe this will mean taking up a hobby, watching a baseball game or gardening. Or maybe it will mean something as simple as soaking in a hot tub at the end of a long day or sleeping late one morning a week. The answers—and the questions—are up to you.

✵ *Which of my responsibilities can I put off until later without doing any harm?* To answer this question, you'll need to examine your systems to see where you can be flexible. What about meetings? Most of us are seriously overinventoried in that area. What are your chances of folding one meeting into another, thereby coming up with a little extra free time? Is there anything you do on a daily basis that you might be able to get away with doing every *other* day?

✵ *What am I doing that someone else could be doing for me?* Quite a few things, most likely. Our nation was founded on the value of individualism, and to this day, many of us pay little attention to matters such as collaborating and delegating. For instance, ask yourself if you're using your assistant or intern as much as you could be. If you are, not only would you be helping yourself, you'd also be improving the experience of your subordinate, who might be getting a tad bored. What about the idea of trading tasks with a coworker? You both surely possess differing strengths and weaknesses. Could you help each other out by switching around a few responsibilities, without compromising either of your positions?

Keep these questions in the forefront of your mind, and return to them frequently to get into the habit of thinking differently. When this happens, you can start prioritizing and working your way toward increased professional and personal satisfaction.

There we have the Seven Guiding Principles. Think about them, look them over carefully, and return to them as needed, but don't expect to start living by them overnight. Some people may need months or even years to internalize the lessons of these principles. Even then, most of us have to be vigilant about old, counterproductive habits creeping back into place. As time progresses, the more you practice living by these principles, the more they'll feel like second nature. When that happens, you'll find yourself appreciating and enjoying a quality of life that you may not have been able to achieve otherwise.

Chapter Reference

Cziksentmihalyi, M. (1991). *The psychology of optimal experience.* New York: HarperCollins.

Chapter 2

Taking Stock

Hotels and motels *must* run smoothly—that is a fact. If they don't, then the flow of guests will soon ebb. That's the reality. One way to ensure a smooth operation is by regularly taking stock of necessary supplies and personnel. Are there enough towels, soap, and shampoo in each room? Is a lifeguard present at the swimming pool and a hostess at the coffee shop?

Running out of essentials is a sign of trouble, and running out of what is essential on a personal basis is a sign of trouble too. To make it in this field over the long haul, you'll need such "essentials" as energy, commitment, motivation, and a good set of systems. The best place to start when taking stock of your personal situation is to learn how to keep track of your time.

We're talking about your day-to-day, hour-to-hour time. Where does it all go? Is it being used well? Do you feel overwhelmed or at loose ends? In this chapter, we provide some simple ways to track how you spend your time. You'll also learn ways to assess what you're actually getting—emotionally, intellectually, spiritually, practically—out of the time you devote to your work and other interests.

But wait a minute, you say. The hotel and motel field is not very conducive to sitting around and reflecting on your day. In fact, you protest, you're lucky if you even get through the day! Okay, we hear you. Granted, there's not a lot of time in any of your given days to reflect. We've already agreed that there's considerable pressure in this business, and that most of you are doing all you can to stay afloat. But you have to admit that "staying afloat" is really not a pleasurable or productive way to live, is it?

One of the most important messages that we hope to convey in this book is that every day of your life is special and deserves to be treated as such. To that end, we urge you to carefully and methodically consider how you spend your time. One way we propose that you do that is by keeping a record or log of all of your daily activities. Keeping a log can be absolutely fascinating, even surprising.

Think about it. Most adults spend at least 16 out of 24 hours a day awake and, to some degree, active. For many of you who are working in the hotel and motel field, those 16 hours of "awake" time can stretch out to 17, 18, or even 19 hours. During that time, a good portion of what we do should be gratifying in some way. Ask yourself whether you are kept busy with activities that engage you intellectually, emotionally, physically, and spiritually. Are you happy and energized as a result of your work? If and when that happens, you probably will experience that sense of flow that we discussed in the previous chapter.

The unfortunate truth, however, is that too many of us spend too much of our time with activities and tasks that offer no flow whatsoever. That leaves us feeling unfulfilled, bored, restless, frustrated, and even anxiety ridden. We start asking ourselves questions such as, what's the point, why bother, or what's in it for me?

We suspect that you, as a hotel and motel professional, know exactly what we're talking about. Sometimes your work really wears you down, doesn't it? When you've got a half-dozen frat boys in a room disturbing other guests and it's your job to quiet them, you're not really feeling that "flow," are you? When a case of Legionnaire's disease threatens to disrupt a convention of 500 guests, there goes another "no-flow" day. And those are just your on-the-job difficulties. The demands of day-to-day life also can be "flow busters."

Consider tasks such as paying bills, doing laundry, grocery shopping, commuting, servicing your car, chauffeuring the kids around, or dealing with the needs of aged parents. Almost all of us endure periods when these tasks feel absolutely relentless. When that happens, it can bring us down to a dispirited place from which we can only escape through a concerted effort to make ourselves feel better. At those times, we have to step back from our problems and convince ourselves that we have more control over our lives than we sometimes feel we do. When we really start to think about how we use our time and how we *feel* about how we use our time, then we can begin to make the necessary changes and adjustments in our schedules. Once we do that, things will start to improve.

One of our goals in writing this book is to help you find the right methods by which to focus on your life in a productive and proactive manner. The kind of intense attention that we urge you to devote to yourself here can ultimately help you. In the long run, it may allow you to simplify what you're doing and thereby make your life and your work more satisfying. To that end, we're going to ask you to do something that may not be easy. We want you to put yourself under a magnifying glass and examine the ways in which you spend your time, to consider how you use the precious minutes and hours of your day—not just at work but also before you leave for work and when you get home. In doing this, you may come to see how the different spheres of your life interface, and then you can make decisions about how you can improve the balance.

During our many conversations with the hotel and motel professionals we interviewed for this book, some people expressed frustration about "not having control of their lives." One story that particularly lodged in our minds was about a fellow, Rudy, who was a director of marketing for a hotel and conference center in Salt Lake City. Rudy grew up on a small family farm and was used to hard work. He worked his way through college and up the ladder in the industry. In the course of all of this hard work, he had let himself become a workhorse. He took on those jobs that would otherwise go unclaimed. As an executive, he had difficulty delegating. Nobody worked as hard as he did, he thought. In fact, Rudy worked so hard that he had neglected developing other areas of his life. At age 34, he still hadn't gotten married or had kids, two things high on his priority list. He didn't get back to Wyoming to see his family much. He had little in the way of outside interests. And he wasn't very good about staying fit. He ate on the run—a lot of highly spiced and salty fast foods—and he didn't exercise. Because of the pressure at his job and a genetic predisposition toward the problem, Rudy developed high blood pressure. His doctor gave him an order: either clean up your act, or you'll face some serious consequences.

Rudy took this warning to heart. He returned to an early love—swimming. In fact, he had been a serious competitive swimmer in high school and college, but as a working adult, he never felt that he could make time for such a pursuit. Now, because of his doctor's orders, he made the time . . . and it made all the difference. Five or six days a week he went to a health club and swam for an hour. Not only did he gain health benefits almost immediately, but he also began to feel as though he had a life away from work for the first time in a long while. He got to know other people who swam at the club. His world opened up a little bit. He started enjoying his work more and being less critical of his staff. He hadn't yet met the woman of his dreams, but he felt more inspired to look for her.

Rudy's story is hardly unique. So many of us become single-minded, even compulsive, in our quest to achieve that we allow our relationships, our physical well-being, and our enjoyment of life to suffer. All it took for Rudy was a dunk in the deep end to get him going again. What might it be for you? A walk in the woods? An evening spent discussing a good book with other people? Playing banjo in a jug band? Ballroom dancing? Pottery? Golf? Maybe it's quality time with the kids, or perhaps just some couch potato time, sitting around with a pint of ice cream and a good movie. Whatever it is you need, hopefully this chapter will teach you how to monitor yourself so that you can tap into your needs and fulfill them before frustration sets in.

 *Keeping Track*

Although we've said it before, we'll say it again—an awful lot gets lost in the shuffle of a typical, busy day. Sometimes the day is even busier than typical. With these kinds of demands on your time, you can expect the more subtle aspects of your day to fade into the background. You may not get to ask yourself questions, consciously or unconsciously, such as, Were you satisfied with your performance? Did you learn anything? Did you have meaningful interactions with other people? It's important to ask these kinds of questions.

For you to develop a real awareness of how you spend your day, and how you *feel* about how you spend your day, we suggest you try the following assignment. Think of this section as a kind of workbook, and grab a pencil and paper. Roll up your sleeves, and let's get to work. A good place to start is by examining the section heads that follow:

- **Start/Stop/Total**
- **Activity**
- **Feelings**
- **Efficiency**
- **What's My Role?**
- **End-of-Day Analysis**

These words and phrases may not mean anything now but in time they will become clear. For now, all you have to do is copy them into a notebook. Choose one that's small enough to carry around easily throughout the day. A small, spiral-bound memo pad is perfect to tuck into a pocket. In this notebook, keep a record of all of your activities. Call it a journal, a log—it should be a detailed account of precisely what you do with your time during any given day.

We fully understand that at times you'll view this activity as just another distraction in your already overwhelming schedule. But our intention is to *simplify* your life. It just might take a little work to get to that point. Keep in mind, however, that the extra time you put into these exercises now is bound to free up time down the line. This journal keeping works especially well if you keep at it for an entire week or longer, because that way you'll get to examine the pattern of your weekends, which, for many of you in this field, are particularly intense.

We recognize that this activity cannot necessarily be your first priority, and that sometimes you'll have to put it on the back burner. When you're in the middle of handling a group of two dozen tourists who have just arrived and whose luggage is missing, this may not be the perfect time to whip out your little notebook and write down, "11:30: Pacifying hysterical tourists." When you manage to come up for air, you can jot down what you've been doing. If possible, when engaged in an activity, try to glance at your watch and make a mental note of the start and finish time. The actual jotting down part can come later. Obviously you should use whichever shorthand methods that will make this work easier for you, since this is for your eyes only.

Start/Stop/Total

It's time to take a good, long look at your day. What kind of day was it? Were you in nonstop meetings? Did you lock horns with a coworker? Were you able to come up with a brilliant, innovative way to save your business a lot of money this year? Did you have the opportunity to make an elderly couple's golden wedding anniversary the stuff of dreams?

Perhaps none or all of the above happened to you today. The specifics are not important. What *is* important is whether anything happened that made you feel good. And what about the stuff you *didn't* feel good about? Missing your child's piano recital. Having a fight with your partner over some petty nonsense. Developing a stress headache after hour upon hour of dealing with problems. How did you handle all of that?

Most people's days are typically like that, with good and bad elements, and more often than not, the bad have a tendency to overrule the good. That's why it's important to get into the habit of paying close attention to your day. Keeping this journal will help you establish that habit.

The sorry truth of modern life is that we all tend to live by the clock, so that's where we will begin. In order for you to take stock of your day, for a while you're going to have to be more of a clock watcher. That means from the moment your alarm goes off in the morning until you close your eyes at night, *you will need to pay attention to what you're doing.*

You'll probably be amazed at first over how you feel. You'll start to discover the myriad things you do in any given day. You may be well aware of getting dressed and walking the dogs and watering the plants, but what about making the kids' lunches, picking up the dry cleaning, checking in on your elderly neighbor . . . the list could go on and on, and everyone's list is different. The point is, our days deserve attention, because without that attention, they can easily become a blur.

The task, then, is to become aware. Each time you begin a new activity, note the "start" time. Do the same when you finish that activity, writing down the "stop" time before you move on to your next activity. And don't forget—*everything* you do in the course of the day should be noted. Isometric exercises at the computer? Write it down. Calling grandma to check in? Write it down. Checking your child's math homework? Down it goes. Later we'll ask you to tally the "total time spent," but you don't have to worry about that at the moment. The important thing right now, in the middle of your crazy day, is to make notes of whatever it is you do—30 minutes for carpooling, 15 minutes to walk Fido, an hour for a training session at work, 20 minutes to meet with the elevator inspector—and then do the math at the end of the day to see where your time went.

Let's hear from your fellow hotel and motel professionals who have "gotten with the program."

👑 I had a lot of resistance to this exercise at first. I have to say that in the beginning I found it a real drag to have to expend energy, which I had too little of to start out with, on looking at my life so closely. It's a little scary to do that. "You mean I've just spent 27 minutes talking to my mother-in-law about what she's going to serve for Easter dinner?" But then the more I did it, the better I started to feel about myself. I started to see patterns emerging where previously I had thought I was in a state of chaos, and I wound up feeling like I really do a pretty good job of keeping all my balls in the air.

👑 The thing about this exercise is that once you start writing things down, in black and white, you really see where your time is going, and that can totally inspire you to start making changes. Take my situation. I'm a banquet sales manager at one of the top hotels in Chicago. I work hard . . . really hard. If I'm lucky, some days I get to have lunch. Otherwise, it's like a power bar on the run. Plus I have a family, so there's a whole other arena of commitments that I have to attend to. When I did this exercise, it naturally made me look at patterns, and one thing that I saw that I didn't really like was how much time I'd spend at night helping Robbie, my 11-year-old, with his homework. Some nights an hour goes into that, and, believe me, it's not quality time. It's pressured, harried time where I feel like I'm being manipulated. Maybe he just wants to spend more time with me, but it's become this very dependent thing where he can't get his work done unless I'm sitting there. So we're working on that, and I'm looking forward to having real quality time with him elsewhere. The point is that this exercise made me aware of the problem and got me to start making some changes.

Sometimes solutions are so simple that you can't see them because they're right in front of you. That's the way it was with me after I did this exercise. The problem, in fact, *was* exercise. I wasn't getting enough of it, and I was feeling this drain on my energy because of it. When I computed my "Start/Stop/Total" time, I saw that I was spending time on commuting at the expense of exercise, and I figured out that I could walk to work three days a week. Sure, it would take me an hour (I could get a ride home though), but that was one less hour for exercise that I'd have to factor into my schedule.

Activity

Moving ahead in your workbook, we come to your next assignment: filling in your **Activity** chart. This is a real revelation for most people who do this for the first time. You'll find yourself in so many guises: manager (coordinate holiday schedules), mediator (bring Fred and Jodie together to iron out last night's problem), troubleshooter (find last-minute babysitter for visiting rock star and spouse), life partner (see lawyer with Kim to draw up living wills), friend to one, some, or many (give baby shower for Lesley), son or daughter (bring in mom's car for snow tires), parent (Jessie's piano recital), neighbor, community activist, home owner, religious group member, hobbyist, athlete, musician, and more. Your **Activity** entries will paint a self-portrait. The more specific your entries, the more detailed your self-portrait.

Remember, the information in your workbook is *for your eyes only.* How you use your time and how you *feel* about how you use your time is your own business. Let's hear from your colleagues on this subject.

I actually wound up having a lot of fun with this activity. I remember showing it to my wife and saying, "Look, honey. Look how much I get done in a day. Aren't I a superman?" And she patted me on the head and said, "Yes, sweetheart. You are. Now here's something else for your chart. Please take out the garbage."

Wow. This was a sobering experience. I'm a room controller, and I like figures, but when I figured out how much of my life was about figures, I figured

I might be a little boring, no? By the time I was finished, I decided I needed a hobby. Something really
fanciful as an antidote to all that. So I got into making
marionettes. Don't ask me why—it's a long story—but
I love it.

Feelings

Now that you've completed the **Start/Stop/Total** and
Activity sections, it's time to start exploring other
aspects, namely, your emotions. Jot down your feelings
about each activity close to the time you undertake it.
The sooner you're able to jot down these feelings, the
more meaningful your notations will be, and the less
likely you are to edit them, either consciously or
unconsciously. Don't feel that you have to make long,
detailed notes. Any and all notations that make sense
to *you* will do. (Again, this is for your eyes only.) It
might help to think in terms of "feeling" words. Are
you happy? Sad? Angry? Bored? Worried? Relieved?
Another useful way to approach the assignment is to
think in terms of opposite feelings, and then figure
out where you fall on the spectrum. Are you leaning
toward happy or sad? Tense or relaxed? Tired or
energized? Interested or disinterested?

The goal of the **Feelings** section is to be able to
gauge the amount of satisfaction you receive from
your various activities. Obviously not every task we
take on is meant to bring us joy and pleasure. Washing
and ironing clothes is not a day in the country for
most people. Going for a check-up is not an occasion
to jump for joy. But even such burdensome tasks

may bring us some measure of satisfaction if their completion allows us to cross them off our "to-do" lists. Even tedious tasks can be less so if you can manage to do two things at once. Maybe you can talk on the phone while you polish your shoes, or learn a little French or Italian from audiotapes while you're ironing. Keeping a log of the various feelings you experience during the day will help you pinpoint the things from which you derive pleasure. If you notice certain patterns emerging—for instance, if music makes a task easier, or if you prefer team activities to solo pursuits—then you'll have discovered something worth knowing about yourself.

Don't feel you have to explore every facet of your feelings before making your notations. Your visceral response—the one that comes straight from the gut—is most likely your best indicator. And don't feel that you have to tiptoe around your feelings or be reluctant to vent because "somebody might see." The only person who's guaranteed to see this, after all, is you. Let's hear from other professionals regarding this area.

This part of the workbook activity was definitely an eye-opener. You really get to find out things about yourself. For instance, meetings are my favorite part of the job. I manage a staff, and while many people regard meetings as a particularly gruesome form of hell, I really like them. I like people, I like problem solving, and the two go hand in hand, as far as I'm concerned.

There's a lot of genetic predisposition toward depression in my family, and so when I started feeling kind of down over a six-month period, I just thought, "Well, there are the genes, catching up with me." But after I got through with this part of the workbook activity and looked at how I allot my time and how I *feel* about how I allot my time, I realized that the thing that made me feel best was spending time with my three-year-old daughter, and the thing that made me feel worst was spending all that time away from her. This activity really helped me clarify my priorities, and I wound up formulating a job-sharing plan with another woman who has a young child. Now we both get to spend more time at home, and we and our kids are doing so much better.

Efficiency

As a hotel and motel professional, surely you appreciate the significance of efficiency. Bungled reservations, meals delivered to the wrong rooms, inventory issues . . . these all add up quickly and problematically. The rule of the game is that disappointed guests are not returning guests. It is enormously difficult to undo a mistake and to repair a negative impression. And nothing transmits as quickly in this field as perceived inefficiency.

How well are you doing in the efficiency department? Are you a flake, or are you a control freak? Do you say one thing and do another? As you consider the issue of efficiency and how it plays out in your day-to-day life, remember that there are situations where efficiency does not necessarily win you brownie points. For instance, when you get home at the end of a long day, it might be less "efficient" if you chop an onion by hand for your dinner, but you might get more satisfaction out of the tactile pleasure connected to the task. Similarly, it might be more "efficient" for you to type a letter to your great-aunt, but you might feel more emotionally connected if you write it by hand. Once again, you are the judge. If you decide that efficiency is not particularly applicable to a certain task, simply write "N/A" (not applicable) in your log. Otherwise, make an effort to rate your efficiency on a 1-to-5 scale for any given activity. Your colleagues relate the following regarding efficiency.

👑 After keeping the log, I was amazed by how inefficient I was in some areas of my life. For instance, I'm always late paying bills, which is entirely unnecessary, because I have the money to pay them, thank goodness. But I just get hung up on stuff, and so I tend to let my bookkeeping slide. After going through this **Efficiency** exercise, I couldn't escape the truth. There it was—just how inefficient I can be—in black and white, and so I decided, on the spot, to turn over a new leaf and get things under control. I'm starting out by doing a lot more automated banking, for one thing.

👑 I imagine that when some people do this exercise, they wind up feeling like they've been falling down on the job. When I did this exercise, I realized that I must be driving people crazy! I've turned into a real bean counter, and I've got to learn to lighten up a little.

What's My Role?

Earlier in this chapter we made the point that all of us, over a 24-hour period, play a variety of roles. We're managers, auditors, food and beverage controllers, engineers, and so on, but we're also husbands, wives, partners, parents, brothers, sisters, sons, daughters, friends, teammates, teachers, coaches, bird-watchers, dog walkers, photographers, surfboarders . . . you name it. Think about which of these roles you like best. For instance, as a concierge, do you enjoy alerting your guests to the glories of your fair city? Do you like the number-crunching part of your job best? Are you particularly turned on by teamwork, training, or design?

Think hard about all of the different roles you play, and then, during a given week, compile a list of these roles in the back of your notebook or pad. As you fill in your log, figure out which roles you've been playing for which activity, but don't feel that you have to write these down close to the time of the activity. This category and the next—**End-of-Day Analysis**—can be filled in when you find some quiet time.

End-of-Day Analysis

Now for the grand finale. The last thing we want you to do each day, just before you turn out the lights, is analyze your log. This is your opportunity to really examine your habits, and the results can be genuinely surprising. Follow these steps:

1. Begin by totaling the first column, **Start/Stop/ Total.** Add up the total for each activity, and note it.

2. Review what you've written in the **Activity** column, and read across the row to **What's My**

	ACTIVITY #1	ACTIVITY #2	ACTIVITY #3
Start Stop Total			
Feelings			
Efficiency			
What's My Role?			

Role? Think about what your role has been in each activity, and note it in the appropriate place.

3. When you've filled in the entire **What's My Role?** column, check back to the **Feelings** column, and think about which roles you found

most pleasurable or satisfying. Note as well those activities you found least pleasurable or satisfying. Give yourself time to think about how you might rearrange your life to maximize time spent in the pleasurable roles and minimize time spent in those roles you do not enjoy.

4. Look back at your **Start/Stop/Total** column, and match it with the **Feelings** column. How much time did you spend doing things that offered you little satisfaction? How much time did you spend doing the things you love the most?

5. Think about what was most surprising in your log, and make a note of it. Perhaps it was how much time you spent doing things that you genuinely do not enjoy. Or, maybe—hopefully— it was the other way around. Maybe you're surprised over how much pleasure you took in the more scientific aspects of your work—the mathematical calculations, for instance. Or maybe you were surprised over how interested you were in the marketing and public relations aspects of your work as a manager.

6. Repeat this process every day for a week, each day with a new log. At the end of the week, review all of your notes, paying special attention to the **End-of-the-Day Analysis.** Give yourself ample time to think about what you are reading.

Again, the goal here is to reflect. Ultimately you want to find enough time in your life to do more of what you love and less of what you don't. To achieve that goal, you must keep track of the following **Seven Guiding Principles,** discussed in Chapter 1.

1. Become an active listener.
2. Think outside of the box.
3. Take time to figure out what you find most satisfying.
4. Create time for the things you care about.
5. Learn to enjoy what's in front of you.
6. Learn to be flexible.
7. Prioritize.

Keeping a log and being mindful of the Seven Guiding Principles is only one step toward making the most of your life as a hotel and motel professional. The next chapter introduces you to the very important issue of organization.

Chapter 3

Everything in Its Place

In the last chapter, we started to talk about the issue of time and how it impacts on your life. We presented you with exercises that would offer you a clearer understanding of how you use your time. In this chapter, we will be discussing organization. As a hotel and motel professional, surely you know how important it is to be organized. Without a high level of organization, a business can soon fall into disorder, and when a hotel or other motel accommodation is in disorder, it puts the consumer in jeopardy. Disorganized hotel professionals can translate into room mix-ups for guests, and that can cause a real hardship for people who come to you with high expectations for holidays and special events. You owe it to them and to yourself to become and stay organized.

Without such a pledge, any other promise will be hollow indeed.

Now you don't have to be a rocket scientist to understand that, almost invariably, there is some kind of connection between time and organization. So many of us speak about being "time poor," "racing against the clock," "being behind the eight ball," and so on. What we're really saying is that time slips through our fingers, and that frustrates us. Well, folks, we're here to help.

Keep in mind that the issue of time and, accordingly, the issue of organization are, to a large degree, culturally impacted. Some societies don't prize efficiency and punctuality as much as others do. In our society, by and large, we hold the values of organization and efficiency in high esteem. In fact, most employers look to hire people whose employment histories bear out these traits. So, as far as we are concerned in this book, we're going to assume that we're all on the same page here, and that we all agree that being organized is a good thing. But, like all good things, too much of a good thing can become a not-so-good thing.

Ask yourself how much you value organization. Will you stop at nothing to make sure that your socks are neatly arranged in your drawers? Do you start to twitch if someone moves the pencils you've lined up so compulsively? Or are you a let-it-all-hang-out type who relies on a string around your finger to remind you of important events?

No matter which end of the spectrum you're closer to, chances are you may feel that you haven't quite gotten the organization thing down yet. Maybe you're running behind, or maybe you're always the first one at the party. Maybe you even get to the party early and have to endure your host's dirty looks! Being organized and managing your time well is part art, part science, and part pure determination. Let's hear what some of your colleagues in the field have to say on this subject.

♛ I lump "organization" together with "efficiency." To me, efficiency is all about setting up systems that work *for you.* They don't have to work for anybody else (except, unfortunately, the person who has to come after you, so make sure you train that person before you leave a job). But what I'm saying is that they don't have to look pretty or elegant or whatever. They just have to work. If that means that you keep paper clips in a paper cup on your desk and it works for you, that's fine. I'm one of four front office clerks at the hotel where I work, and all of us do things differently from each other. We're not cut out by cookie cutters. But I have to say that we all do a good job, and there aren't too many details that fall through the cracks.

♛ When you're really organized, what you do comes to feel like second nature. Imagine an athlete. He doesn't have to think about how to move his body when he hits a ball. His body *knows* what to do. That's the way I feel when I'm really organized. I don't have to lose a lot of precious time *thinking* about what I have to do. I just *know.*

♛ Being organized and efficient makes repetitive tasks bearable. I mean, if you had to really think each time you filed away a piece of paper, you'd probably start tearing your hair out in no time.

🪰 Being organized is like being in the groove. You're trucking along, it feels good, you've got the rhythm, and everything's all right with the world.

🪰 I refuse to let time rule my life. You know, in this field, the great educational model is the Swiss hotel school. And what do you think of when you think of the Swiss? That's right—watches! And cuckoo clocks! Which is enough to make a person cuckoo! I don't want to live in a way that I have to account for every minute of every day. Life's too short for that.

🪰 My father was in the military, and time was always this big deal in our family. We had to synchronize our watches—I'm not kidding—and he used to go by military time. Dinner at 1800 hours and all that. Fortunately, as much as I love my father, I don't live in his house anymore, and I don't have to think about time as a tyrant. I have a perfectly well-developed sense of time that I carry around inside of me, and I think that's a much saner way to live. I get up the same time every morning, without an alarm clock, and guess what? I *never* oversleep, and I'm *never* late!

Time Management

You know that song that's been a hit for everyone from the Rev. Al Green to the Dave Matthews Band—"Ain't It Funny How Time Slips Away?" Well, it's a great song, all right, but when you come down to it, it really is *not* so funny how time slips away. Learning how to manage your time, and how to avoid the pitfalls of wasted time, is a big priority for all of you who are working in the pressured world of the hotel and motel industry.

Time is a fact of life—as fundamental as the weather—but our feelings about it can be extremely complicated. The issue of time and how it impacts on us and those around us is often confusing, frustrating, and even infuriating. People who are chronically late try the patience of friends, family, and coworkers. In fact, many people who are chronically late are said to be "passive-aggressive," meaning that they seem, on the surface, to be agreeable to the desires and needs of other people, but they are actually passively resisting them in a way that can be quite hostile. Being chronically late, forgetting important things—these are classic hallmarks of passive-aggressive behavior.

If we agree that time is a complicated and even a thorny issue, then how can we tame it? There are a number of ways to go about it. Some good ideas from your colleagues follow:

👑 You're not going to get anywhere in terms of controlling your time until you can learn how to say the most important word in the English language: No. Too many of us have a real problem with the "N" word, and, as a result, we take on way too much and wind up really doing a number on ourselves. I'm an assistant banquet sales manager, and the woman I work for is brilliant, but she's a total workaholic. She doesn't have a life outside of the job. I do—a very nice life, thank you—and I've had to learn how to control the demands she makes on me. It hasn't been easy, but learning how to say no is the most important lesson I've ever mastered.

🦅 Some of us handle interruptions better than other people. I'm one of those who don't do interruptions well at all. When I'm doing something important, whether it's on the job or at home, I have to close myself off from distractions. I'll have my phone machine on, for instance, and I just won't answer the phone. Now that drives my mother crazy—*What if it's an emergency?*—but all I can say is that I'll just have to take my chances.

🦅 I find that a really useful way to think about time is that every minute counts. When some people finish a task and they've got lunch coming in 15 minutes, they'll say, "Oh, why bother starting something now?" But when I finish a task and I've got 15 minutes till lunch, I'll say, "I've got 15 minutes to get something done." Maybe it's just a few little odds and ends—business matters, like confirming a date for a meeting or checking out some information on the Internet, or personal stuff, like making a restaurant reservation for dinner or phoning another mother to invite her daughter to your daughter's birthday party. Whatever. Surely you can find *something* to fill 15 minutes.

🦅 A great way to approach time is to think about your day as one big trip. It's like you're going from New York to Boston and everything you do should be plotted

Just Say No

Learning to say no is an acquired skill for many of us. Until we master that skill, we can't expect to manage our time as we would hope to. Here are some valuable pointers with regard to the art of saying no:

🔱 Feel the power of the word. Say it. *No.* Try to stay away from constructions such as, "I'd rather not," or, "If it's all the same to you, I'd prefer to try it another way." Use the powerful "N" word.

🔱 It helps to be really sure what you think before you give your "no" answer. You don't want it to be tentative. If you need more time to think something over, then ask for it.

🔱 Some people are really bad at hearing "no." Just remember—that's *their* problem, not yours. Repeat the word—as many times as necessary—until it gets through to them. If it still doesn't work and others keep badgering you, then maintaining silence or changing the topic of conversation may be called for.

🔱 It's hard to disappoint another person, and you may want to acknowledge that disappointment when you say no to someone. But that shouldn't change your answer.

🔱 You may want to offer a compromise—that's up to you. If your boss asks you to stay an extra two hours, maybe you'll want to say, "I can't do two hours tonight, but I can give you 45 minutes."

> ⚜ Back up your "no" with body language. Shaking your head is a universally understood signal.
>
> ⚜ Be brief and to the point when you say no. If your boss asks you to stay late, you might say, "I told you last week that I needed to leave early tonight because it's my son's championship basketball game." You don't have to go into any further explanations or justifications. You're not on trial.

out to make sense geographically. You wouldn't run a delivery down to Providence and then out to Connecticut and then back to Long Island, would you? You'd look at your route, and you'd plot out your stops in a way that has some logic to it. So when I look at my "to-do" list and I see I've got dry cleaning to drop off and my new eyeglasses to pick up and this and that, I plot out a route that also has logic, so that I'm not running circles around myself.

⚜ Being a "do-it-yourselfer" might make sense when it comes to building birdhouses or crocheting doilies, but it may not make much sense at all in the overall scheme of your life. I'm a rooms controller for a large hotel in Santa Fe, and my work hours often splash over into my personal time. In other words, I'm time poor. I decided a long time ago that it made more sense for me to conserve my time and energy for work tasks and let other people help me out in the nonwork areas of my life. So instead of hanging on the line with the airlines, for instance, I always use a travel agent. Even when I couldn't afford it very well, I hired someone to clean my house every other week. I shop on the Internet or use merchants who pick up and deliver so I don't have to use up my free time driving around to stores. It's just a kind of mind-set, but you'd be amazed at how much easier it is to live that way.

✦ You can often find time just by analyzing your immediate workspace. Check the layout around you. Are you using up precious seconds or minutes reaching and stretching for things? Your computer, your files, your phone should all be within a mere swivel of your chair.

✦ Plan ahead. It's a great ticket to time-saving. For instance, I always lay out my next day's clothes the night before. Similarly, if I know I have a check to deposit the next day, I'll put the check in my handbag. Same with theater tickets. Let's face it—there are always a million odds and ends to take care of, so this kind of system keeps me from forgetting important stuff.

✦ Making phone calls, even routine ones, can eat up a huge amount of time, so try to return calls to people when they might be inclined to talk less. Take my situation, for instance. I'm in the marketing department of a large hotel chain, and one of the freelancers we work with is terrific and happens to be a major talker. I have a heck of a time getting off the phone with her, so I'll call her at odd hours when I figure she may not be there, like early in the morning or at lunchtime, and I'll be able to leave a message.

⚜ As a general manager of a spa in the Berkshire mountains of Massachusetts, I never have less than a million things to do. One thing I realized I definitely did *not* want to do in my spare time was to use up precious moments talking on the phone with telemarketers. So I registered with the National Do Not Call Registry at <http://www.donotcall.gov>. I suggest you do the same. You'll immediately start to see a drop-off of harassing calls, particularly at dinnertime, and if people don't stop bothering you, they can be severely fined.

⚜ I like to think of time as a gift that I can give to someone. After all, it's very precious, isn't it? Even in the busiest day, when I'm dealing with the needs of 500 sci-fi fans who have just landed in town for an international convention, I can usually find a few minutes. So let's imagine my father just got back from a vacation to Pebble Beach and he calls up and wants to talk to me about the 18 holes he played there. Okay, this may not be my idea of what I need to hear in the middle of a busy day, but the man is my father, after all, so I'll give him the "gift" of time. I'll say something like, "You've got 10 minutes, dad. Let's do it!" He never seems to mind and, in fact, he usually winds up sticking to his quota.

Making Lists

Now that we've been talking in general ways about how to stay on top of the time issue, let's look at some specific strategies. One of the most important ways to find time is to make and keep lists.

You're not a "list" type of person? Okay, we can respect that. Maybe you don't like to think of yourself as a buttoned-down type. You're more the "free, fresh, wind-in-your-hair" kind of personality. That's fine, and in some areas of life, such people do well, or even better than well. But most people have to march to a certain drummer, at least to some extent. When the boss expects us to be somewhere at a certain time, we'd better be there. When a deadline looms, we'd better meet it.

Besides, the point of making lists is to make your life easier. Compare it to going on a road trip to some place you've never been before. You wouldn't set out without a map or some kind of written directions, would you? Or what about going grocery shopping? Would you keep it all in your head? "Okay, let me see. Ed wants veggie burgers, and Carrie wants fruit roll-ups, and I think we need some shampoo . . ." Uh-uh. Doesn't make sense, does it? Not only would you want a list, but if you're familiar with the supermarket, you might even want to have a list that concentrates all of your purchases by respective areas. That is, you group all of your dairy items together, and all of your produce items together, and so forth. That will keep you from running from aisle 1 to aisle 6 and back to aisle 1 to aisle 4, taking two or three times as long as it has to!

A good to-do list—which is what we're advocating here—not only reminds you of what you need to do but organizes you in the bargain. Maintaining this list goes a long way toward moving your days from chaos to control. Whether you use a memo pad, a pocket calendar, an electronic organizer, a stick-it pad, or a ball-point pen on the palm of your hand, you won't want to leave home without it. And once you start keeping this daily list, you also may find that a weekly or even a monthly list is helpful as well. Let's hear from your colleagues on this subject.

The very first item on my to-do list is "Review My List." It's how I start off every day. I'll make myself some coffee and I'll sit down in the kitchen, before the rest of the family gets up, and in that quiet time, I'll spend five minutes carefully looking over my list. Once I have that big picture in mind—and remember, it only takes five minutes—I feel like I have a plan for my day, and I feel a lot more on top of things.

You know how they say you should always keep your résumé on one page? The same holds true for your to-do list. If your list runs more than one page, then there's too much "to do" on your to-do list. I'm a general manager for a hotel in Branson, Missouri, and I'm always telling my staff, "Hey, folks. If *I* can keep it to a page, why can't you?"

Some people do crossword puzzles in ink. Frankly, I've never understood those people. I guess they're a lot better than I am. I'm a pencil person, and the same is true when it comes to my to-do list. I don't like to look at a lot of cross-outs. It makes me feel inadequate.

To-do lists are not cast in stone. They're meant to be flexible. We're only human. That means that things get canceled and shuffled around, and you mustn't allow yourself to get all hung up on it.

🐝 Before I went into the hotel business, I was a jazz singer. As a singer, I learned that one of the most important elements in music is silence. It can surprise, it can reinforce, it can relieve. Similarly, on your to-do list, one of the most important elements is "nothing." In other words, factor in some "nothing"—otherwise known as "free time"—into your day. Believe me, you're going to need it. Something always comes up unexpectedly—car trouble; your cat has babies; you leave a bag in a taxi—and if you factor in some free time, then you'll have some wiggle room when you need it.

🐝 Checking off your to-do list as you go along is one of life's great pleasures. Just put a nice fat line through each item as you complete it, and luxuriate in the feeling of accomplishment.

🐝 I got so good at keeping a daily to-do list that I figured I'd start keeping a weekly to-do list as well. That way, I can try to get organized for bigger chunks of time. Now if I have something important due 10 days ahead, I can see it coming. Next step is the monthly list!

🐝 Making lists is all well and good, but you can't really hope to do that effectively until you understand the principles of prioritization.

Organizers

Frankly, it's hard for us to imagine a high-functioning professional in the hotel and motel field who doesn't make use of an organizer. There may be some geniuses

Prioritization

The organizational principle of *prioritization*—attacking tasks in the order of their importance—is critical when making lists. Some prioritization tips follow:

🦚 A to-do list doesn't make sense unless you prioritize it. You need to put the most important thing at the top of your list.

🦚 To figure out priorities, consider the items on the list and ask yourself what good or bad things might happen if you do or don't complete the items.

🦚 Always finish one task before you go on to the next.

🦚 Keep in mind that priorities shift—even in the course of any given day. It's fine to put something at the top, but then, as the day goes along, if you see that its importance has become less pressing, feel free to shift it to a lower position.

out there who carry it all in their heads, but we haven't come across them.

Recommending an organizer can be a tricky affair. Different people have very different styles, which will impact upon their choice. Are you technologically challenged? Do you tend to lose things? Have you been relying on the back of napkins all of these years, and do you want to ease yourself into the whole organizational thing? These are questions to ask yourself, but while you do, let's hear what your colleagues in the field have to say.

☙ Some people like calendars that are basically a day at a time, others a week at a time. Me, I like to be able to see a month at a time, because I'm a big-picture sort of person, so I back up my week-at-a-glance calendar with a hanging monthly calendar in my office.

☙ How can anyone *not* use an electronic organizer these days? I run a bed-and-breakfast (B&B) on the coast of Maine, which may sound pretty low-key to you, but frankly I don't know how I'd survive without my electronic organizer. Whether it's a Palm Pilot® or a Handspring® or any of the knockoffs, to me the difference between an electronic organizer and a regular old date book is like the difference between a computer and a typewriter. My electronic organizer allows me to program in birthdays and anniversaries and all that, as well as information about guests, vendors, advertising outlets, and other important contacts in my life. You can also set alarms for yourself through the day to remind yourself of things—check-in and checkout time, or whatever. It's fantastic!

☙ There's so much hype these days on electronic organizers, but frankly I'm no great fan of them. Call me old-fashioned, but I prefer a good old legal pad on which to jot down my to-dos. It works just fine, and I buy them for next to nothing.

☙ As a general manager, I naturally have a lot on my plate, so I like to cover all my bases. That means I use a desk calendar, an electronic organizer, and a computer calendar. The only hitch with this system is that you've got to make sure that all your calendars are coordinated.

The Lost and Found of Time

Organization seems to breed more organization. In a sense, it's a kind of worldview. Once you get in the mode, before you know it you start coming up with all kinds of ways to save time. We can all can save hours a week just by becoming aware of certain shortcuts. The following tips will give you some ideas in all of the different areas of your life for ways to start owning your time again.

Travel

As a professional in a field that has so much to do with travel and tourism, it is very likely that you yourself may do quite a bit of traveling. Some useful organizing tips from colleagues to ease your business travel follow:

👑 I always keep a master checklist of my travel needs handy. On this list, I can check off whether or not I have my alarm clock, money belt, allergy pills, hand lotion, and so on. I keep a bunch of photocopies of the list on hand, and each time I take a trip, I pull out one of the copies and start taking inventory. It's really helped me not to forget important items.

The incidence of lost or misplaced luggage is going up, up, up. Whenever you pack a suitcase, write down a "receipt" of everything that you've put into it. That way, if your luggage is lost, you'll know what's missing, and you can act on it immediately.

Do yourself a favor—restrict your luggage to one carry-on bag if you possibly can. That way, you can skip the long waits at the carousel and the running after the airlines when they lose your bags.

Get a good map and a road guide to wherever you're going *before* you get there. Maps can be difficult to obtain. You don't want to get stuck. At the very least, print out directions to all of your meetings on Mapquest (<http://www.mapquest.com>) before you leave.

I like to bring my own pillow with me when I travel. That way, I know I can get a good night's sleep. I also throw a night-light into my bag. I've stayed in hotels where the rooms are pitch black at night, and I don't feel like breaking my neck (or my shins) in the dark.

Keep all your receipts together if you're going to be putting in for reimbursement or claiming deductions for tax purposes.

Always carry an extra pair of eyeglasses with you . . . assuming you need eyeglasses.

If you're staying at a hotel that has a dedicated business center, try to reserve a room in that section. Not only will your room probably come with dual telephone/modem lines, fax machines, and free local calling, but you're more likely to be placed away from vacationing college students and crying babies.

Good Habits Start at Home

Are you super-organized at work, but sloppy once you get home? Keep in mind that your disorganization on the domestic front can impact on other areas of your life, no matter how hard you try to segregate things. Some ideas from your fellow professionals about "home improvement" follow:

What drives me nuts more than anything in the world? Losing stuff! Misplacing stuff! Wasting precious time searching in jacket pockets and under sofa cushions for stuff that I would know exactly where it was if I put it in the same place every time. You know what I'm talking about—your wallet, your keys, your eyeglasses, the check you were supposed to deposit. Well, after so many years of aggravation, I've learned my lesson. Now when I get home at night, I put my keys on the key holder in the kitchen, my wallet in the coat pocket of a particular coat in my closet, and so on. Everything has a place of its own, and not looking for stuff has improved the quality of my life 100 percent.

Holding on to junk is a huge obstacle to organization. I make a point of going through closets and drawers at least once a year and divesting myself of things I don't need. Outfits I'm never going to fit into again, books I have no interest in reading, broken stuff that I tell myself I'm going to fix, but I know it's never going to happen—you know what it's like. I make donations to organizations of stuff that's worthwhile, and I make donations to the dump of stuff that's no good to anybody. Cleaning the debris out of your life is the quickest and straightest path to real organization.

✦ My key to being organized is to have one secret place in my house—one big closet—that's a total mess. It's where I put all the stuff I don't know what to do with, but that I'm not ready to throw away.

✦ I like to keep a wastebasket in every room. That encourages throwing away stuff you don't need.

✦ Whenever I leave a room to go to another room, I pick up something that doesn't belong there, and I take it to where it does belong. With kids in the house, I'm never at a loss to find something that's in the wrong place.

✦ Unread magazines make me feel guilty, so I leaf through them, clip out the one or two articles I might really be interested in, stick them in a standing file, and then toss the rest of it.

✦ I keep cheap vacuums on every level of the house. It translates into less work for me.

. . . And Even More Ways to Save Time

Once you get into the habit of being an organized person, you'll see how many ways there are to become increasingly better at arranging your time. Some suggestions from your colleagues follow:

✦ The thing that's really been a lifesaver for me is the Internet. I do most of my shopping on it. All I do is click a mouse, and then a few days later, there in the mail I've got bank checks, pharmaceuticals, underwear . . . you name it. It's awesome not to have to drive and wait on line at places.

🦋 If you're a commuter, as most of the world is, you really ought to try to make the most of your commute. Since I'm in the car a lot, I do my "reading" by listening to books on tape. In fact, in recent years, it's the only way I've been able to "read." I'm also thinking about dictating notes to myself as I drive. Just sitting there in traffic doesn't do it for me.

🦋 One way to get organized in your life is to relax your standards in certain areas. I'm a very detail-oriented sort of personality, you might even say obsessive, and when I was that way at work *and* at home, it was driving everyone a little crazy. Then I learned to lighten up a little. I've come to realize that if I don't make the beds one morning, the whole world won't come to an end.

🦋 Here's how I've arranged things on the home front: I've got my daily tasks, like making dinner or doing a little shopping, my weekly tasks, like getting my recyclables together, my monthly tasks, like pulling the sofa out from the wall and cleaning behind it, and then there are my yearly tasks, like turning the mattresses or cleaning the grout, but we're not going to worry so much about those.

🦋 Everyone's talking about multitasking these days, and you really should keep it in mind. Do the exercise bike while you read your reports. Talk to your mother while you're ironing. Thinking that way allows you to find extra time all over the place. You'll see what a difference it makes.

Organization is a key principle in making the most of your potential, but it's hardly the whole story. In the next chapter, we will be talking about another talent you'll need to develop: becoming a team player.

Chapter 4

Go, Team!

What is teamwork? It is a powerful force that can move you along the road to achievement. Many famous people have shared their thoughts on the subject of teamwork. Some of their observations are well worth committing to memory:

- "We must all hang together, or, assuredly, we shall all hang separately."—*Founding Father Benjamin Franklin.*
- "Teamwork is the ability to work together toward a common vision. It is the fuel that allows common people to attain uncommon results."—*Nineteenth-century industrialist Andrew Carnegie.*

- "Individual commitment to a group effort—that's what makes a team work, a company work, a society work, a civilization work."—*Football legend Vince Lombardi.*

Teamwork is a word that we hear everywhere today. Go to any motivational meeting and you're liable to encounter a PowerPoint presentation flashing the message TEAM = Together Everyone Achieves More. Walk through the offices of companies all over the country and you'll probably see posters stating, "Teamwork: Simply stated, it is less me and more we."

Teamwork is considered a kind of magic bullet that can rescue American businesses, but, in fact, this regard for teamwork is actually something fairly new to our culture.

Think about it: America was traditionally a society that placed the greatest value on rugged individualism. We honored the mythic Western hero—John Wayne, Clint Eastwood—who rode in and out of town alone. Being called an "individualist" was the highest form of praise, as opposed to those poor souls who made up "a nation of sheep." These were followers who would go with the flow, finding it easier to do what they were told to do rather than think things through themselves.

The extraordinary economic success of postwar Japan was an important factor in changing the way American businesses viewed teamwork. Japan—the first country to be credited with incorporating concepts of teamwork into the workplace—began doing this in earnest in the 1960s, when it set up *quality circles* to ensure the excellence of its products. The quality circles, of which there came to be more than a million in Japan, with more than 10 million members, were made up of employees who met weekly or monthly to discuss any problems of quality that they saw in their output and to collectively generate new ideas for improvement. The concept was a huge success, and by 1970, this Japanese notion of teamwork was transported to the United States, when Lockheed Aircraft utilized it.

Before we go any farther, it is important to define our terms. What exactly do we mean by a "team"? The definition we prefer is a "group of people who work together toward a common task." Take note that a team is more than just a group. A group of people riding a bus together is not a team. But if that bus is stranded in the desert, and if the group pulls together to survive, forming strategies and developing plans, then this group might become a team.

The magic that happens when a group starts to pull together to form a team is directly linked to a force called "synergy." Synergy is a concept that big business also has paid a lot of attention to in recent years, but even though it's trendy, it isn't new. Mark Twain identified it more than a century ago when he wrote that synergy is the "bonus that is achieved when things work together harmoniously." In today's professional vocabulary, the term *synergy*, which comes from the Greek *sunergia*, meaning "cooperation," signifies the combined efforts of two or more parts of a system so that the combined effect is greater than the sum of the efforts of the individual parts. In business and technology, synergy is the effect that comes about when different people, different departments, or even different companies work together to stimulate new ideas that result in greater productivity and achievement.

Every team goes through a fairly prescribed set of stages. Think of it as the "life cycle" of the team. These stages may incorporate the following:

Coming together. The formation of a team can be very of-the-moment or very premeditated. The steps of this first stage commonly include general orientation, setting goals and identifying expectations, and laying the ground rules for personal interaction.

Coming apart. Here we're talking about *conflict.* Factoring in ways to deal with the inevitable conflicts that arise in a team setting is an important second stage in the life of the team.

In the groove. In this stage, the team is clicking along. When a conflict arises, members deal with it quickly and effectively. All members' opinions are heard and taken into account. "Coaching" occurs, with teammates helping each other with their tasks.

The payoff. Here we see the beneficial effects of teamwork in action: higher productivity, increased job satisfaction, less tension, and new ideas.

Change. Nothing stays the same. Look at the major league ball teams, for instance. No matter how many pennants or World Series they win, managers may jump ship, players may be traded, some may retire, and others may be suspended. Some variation of this is exactly what happens on every team, as old members may depart, new members may arrive, projects may be abandoned, and so on.

As an individual working in the hotel and motel industry, you're bound to become part of a team. You may be working in a highly structured corporate setting, where your job is clearly defined and described, as is the way you interface with your employers and fellow workers. Or you may be in a much more intimate setting—an independent hotel or inn, let's say, where you are one of a dozen full-time employees. Even in what may feel like a "one-person" show—a B&B perhaps—aspects of teamwork may still factor into the operation, as you deal with part-time help you hire or vendors, merchants, or service people. Some occupations don't require much attention to teamwork, but in the hotel and motel field, you are continually thrown together with people, thus teamwork counts for a lot.

Communication Is Central

Your team might be lucky enough to have the best players in the world—the strongest, fastest, and smartest that money can buy—but if you all don't know how to talk to each other, then what good is it?

The starting place for getting people to work together—*as a team*—is to instruct them in the basics of constructive communication. Without that, mistakes are bound to happen. Making mistakes is inevitable in

What Position Do You Play?

On a team, each member has a function. Even though we may be identified by our job titles—assistant banquet sales manager, director of transient sales, night audit manager, front desk supervisor—we also come to be known by the roles we play within the team setting. These roles don't have titles, but they are very real and most of us wind up being cast as one of the "types" that follow. Which one best describes you?

The gatherer. This individual is a real workhorse who brings important information and data to the team. Considered very dependable, the gatherer can sometimes get bogged down with details, not "seeing the forest for the trees." Still, a good pick for your team.

The partner. This individual really understands the essence of collaboration. He or she is not looking to steal credit for things, but imparts his or her knowledge to anyone who asks for it and is not afraid of being diminished by asking others for help. He or she is flexible, ready for anything, full of good ideas, and very goal directed.

The listener. This is the team member you go to with a problem. She or he has a marvelous facility for hearing what you have to say, and her or his skills with conflict resolution, building consensus, and other vital matters are invaluable. This person is relaxed, easygoing, cheerful, considerate, and often blessed with a good sense of humor.

🐾 *The challenger.* At times, this individual may be perceived as difficult, overly exacting, and critical, but the fact is, you wouldn't trade him or her for the world. He or she tells it like it is, and when the methods, goals, or ethics of the team may be on shaky ground, this person is not afraid to point it out.

Of the above, none of these "types" is better or worse than the other. Each plays a crucial role on the team. Figuring out which role you play is a big step toward playing it well.

life and in business, but some are less costly than others. Making *a lot* of mistakes in the hotel and motel profession—or even making just one or two—can have a profound impact on your workplace and on you personally. If you tell someone to clear the snow from the sidewalk in front of the hotel, for example, and if he or she doesn't hear you and a guest falls and breaks a leg, then that can result, these days, in a huge lawsuit. In that kind of situation, you'll have to see where the communication breakdown occurred. Don't assume it happened with the other person. It could very well have been your fault. In any event, let's hear what your fellow hotel and motel professionals have to say on this subject.

🐾 I'm the director of food and beverage for a hotel and conference center in Scottsdale, Arizona. As you can imagine, it's a big job, with a great deal of responsibility, and a large cast of characters that reports directly to me. There's the director of catering, along with the senior catering manager and the banquet manager and the banquet setup supervisor, and we've got the beverage manager, with the purchasing supervisor and the storeroom supervisor under him, and the executive chef, with the sous chef and the banquet chef and the restaurant chef and the chief steward, and then there's the director of restaurants, with the restaurant managers and the lounge managers . . . well, you get the idea. That's a lot of players on the field, but the point is that early on in my job I made a cardinal rule that everybody was entitled to a voice. There had to be total equality when it came to communication. That doesn't mean that there's going to be equality in terms of the ultimate decision making—I'm the manager, and the buck stops with me—but everyone is entitled to be heard, and that's an absolute.

I'm a reservations agent in a hotel in New York City, and I report to my reservations manager. She's a good person in most respects and "talks" a good game when it comes to communication, but the fact is she never *stops* talking, and you can't get a word in edgewise with her. She'll start telling you about her trip to Russia, and by the time she's finished, she's somehow wound up in British Columbia. It's exhausting and frustrating, and I haven't figured out what to do about it.

I've been in this business for 30 years. I started as a bellhop in Chicago, and now I'm the general manager of a five-star resort in Southern California. I know what it's like to be the new kid on the block, and I know how much there is to learn. I always start, with these new kids, talking about communication. And one of the first things I point out is that a lot of communication goes on without anything spoken at all. In fact, spoken communication is sort of the tip of the iceberg. You have to be sensitive to the facial expressions and body language of your fellow workers, and especially of your customers. If you've got someone who's tapping on the front desk, how does that translate? When someone shakes his head or rolls his eyes, what's being "said"? My people need to know that unspoken communication can telegraph even more quickly than spoken communication does.

As director of group sales for a chain of 12 hotels in the Midwest, I enjoy quite a bit of interface with the public. In fact, I speak fairly often to groups, both internally and to the "outside world." People can't believe that I had a stuttering problem when I was a kid. Now that's a tough one to overcome, but we all need to analyze the way we actually speak. The quality of our voices is a big determinant in the success of our communication. People who mumble, for instance, can be a major turnoff. Speaking in a monotone is another no-no. If you're a reservationist, for instance, and someone calls you up to book a room and your tone of voice is so monotonous that you could make April in Paris sound boring, then you have to expect that you're going to lose your share of bookings. A loud, grating, shrill voice is another one that many people run away from. So are you guilty of any of the above? Ask yourself that, or better yet, ask a friend that you know will be honest with you. If the diagnosis is not so good, don't despair. You can always find ways to improve your delivery. Some of our greatest actors started out sounding worse than you do!

The Art of Listening

Speaking clearly and slowly, with an appropriate emphasis on certain words and a lively, engaged feeling, will take you far in your journey to success. Just as important, however, is your ability to listen. Let's hear from your colleagues regarding the art of listening.

👑 Communication is all about back-and-forth and taking turns. First, one person talks, and the other listens. Then there's a switch. The key thing, though, is to realize that listening is not a passive activity. You don't just sit there, like you're a piece of furniture in the room. Your listening must appear fully engaged and responsive if you want to get high marks in the communication department. That means nodding your head at appropriate intervals and responding with an occasional "yes," or "I see," or "really?" And, above all, asking appropriate, related questions. I'm the director of human resources for a chain of residential suites in Canada, and my big thing, when I'm interviewing someone, is that if a candidate doesn't ask questions with regard to the things I've said, then I feel like he or she is not in the same room with me. Then it's time for me to say, "Next!"

🦅 Listening is a skill, just like any other skill. You can become a better bridge player if you practice a lot and study, or a better golfer, or a better ballroom dancer. Same with listening. The more you practice and the more you reflect on the art of listening, the better you'll become at it. There are all kinds of techniques you can learn and use.

Listening Techniques

Two of the most useful listening techniques are *reflective listening* and *mirroring*. Here's how they work:

🦅 *Reflective listening.* With this technique, the listener paraphrases the words of the speaker in an attempt to clarify and further understand the content. The reflection allows the speaker to hear her or his words and make the necessary alterations, corrections, and adjustments. "I will be arriving on January 24," says the speaker. "You will be arriving on January 24," replies the listener. "No! I meant February 24," says the speaker, having had the words reflected back to her.

🦅 *Mirroring.* With this technique, you match the other person's posture, movements, mannerisms, level of enthusiasm, and so on. This way you physically reflect in the way that the reflective listening verbally reflects, and in doing so, you strengthen the communication bond.

🐚 Before I went into the hotel business—I'm a concierge in Beverly Hills—I was a reporter for a small-town newspaper. I loved journalism, but I was making next to nothing. Still, I have to say I learned some very valuable lessons from that experience, several of which have to do with listening. As a journalist, you're regularly in the position of interviewing people, and you quickly learn the "do's and don'ts" of listening. For example, when the other person is talking, you don't spend that time thinking about what your next question ought to be. You don't rehearse what you're going to say next. You don't try to impress someone with how well connected you are, what a great vocabulary you have, how funny you are, or anything like that. The idea is to be natural and to focus on the other person.

🐚 As far as I'm concerned, honesty is the best policy, and that honesty has to start with yourself. I know, for instance, that I have a problem when it comes to listening. I suffer from what's called "selective attention." I'm fine if it's just me and another person in an office setting, or even over coffee at a diner, let's say, but if I'm at a party and somebody's trying to talk to me, I can't help myself from looking and listening everywhere else. Once I was looking around the room when somebody was talking to me and that person said, "I'm sorry I'm boring you." I practically melted into a puddle, I was so embarrassed! After that, I've always made it a point to really try to focus in on whomever I'm talking to. I look into the other person's eyes, I move my chair close—whatever it takes to send the message that I'm here for that person and no one else.

 Don't assume that when somebody doesn't seem to be listening to you they're being rude or insensitive. I made just that kind of assumption with a coworker, and then it turned out that he was deaf. I don't mean profoundly deaf, but I later found out that he definitely has a significant hearing deficit. Well, I felt pretty bad to have jumped to conclusions like that.

 Listening is important, but so is picking the right time to try to have a conversation. As a general manager for a hotel in Louisville, Kentucky, I've got days where I'm up to my elbows in problems. That's when I'll inevitably have somebody come running into me with a brilliant idea for why we should change the color scheme of the lobby or what have you. Now you can be a great speaker and a great listener, but if you don't do a very good job of picking your times to speak and listen, then what's the point?

Personality and Attitude

In determining the value you bring to a team, your personality and attitude will be every bit as important as your communication skills. Your personality is like your thumbprint—you're not going to be able to change it—but the good news is that you *can* work on your attitude. In the hotel and motel industry—a field where you will be interfacing on a regular basis with the public—your personality and attitude are particularly significant. Let's hear what your colleagues have to say on the subject:

❦ Most of us, when we hear the word "personality," tend to think in terms of *extroverted*—outgoing and social—or *introverted*, meaning private and reserved. There is some truth that personalities seem to fall into one or the other of those camps, but what some people don't realize is that you can be introverted and yet still have a positive, healthy attitude toward other people. You can also be extroverted and be cynical and contemptuous of others. So don't get down on yourself for what your personality is. Concentrate instead on the kind of attitude you bring to the party.

❦ My parents were pretty old-fashioned types. They believed in wearing a smile, in honesty and loyalty, in putting on a good face to the world, in the virtues of hard work and perseverance. I guess what I'm saying is that they were very big on values, and I think that the value training I got, which became such a big part of my personality and my attitude, has served me well in life.

❦ We live in a society that glorifies those who talk the loudest, like those shock jocks on call-in radio shows. Well guess what? When you go out into the real world and you have to deal with real people, you start to see, very quickly, that those tactics will get you nowhere fast. Quieter values like tact and discretion and minding your own business and knowing how to keep a secret go a lot further in group situations than always saying what's on your mind and complaining and gossiping.

🐝 I really feel that personalities and attitudes can change as a person gets older. I'm a catering manager, and I've got a bunch of youngsters working for me, and when I look at them, I sometimes say to myself, "That's what I used to be like." Then I say, "Thank goodness I'm not like that anymore." Really, every little thing you say to them sets them off. I tell them, "Don't make a Shakespearean tragedy out of everything. If someone says something to you that you don't like, let it roll off your back. Life's too short." The problem is that when you're young, life doesn't seem short. What's the expression? "The trouble with youth is that it's wasted on the young"? Well put!

🐝 I'm the director of human resources for an international hotel chain. I deal with all kinds of people and all kinds of problems, and when I can spot an opportunity to teach someone how to get along better with their coworkers, I pounce on it. One of the techniques I like to tell people about is *reframing*. It's a great attitude adjuster. Basically what it means is putting a new spin on a situation. So let's say your boss jumps on you for being a day late on an assignment. Now keep in mind that there's been a flu epidemic that has created a real manpower shortage, and every able-bodied person in your office, of which you are one, has been working overtime, so your first response is to fume at how ungrateful your boss is. But then you start to reframe. You tell yourself that he's not usually like this. Maybe he's just having a bad day. Maybe *he's* coming down with the flu! This kind of thinking, which is related to rationalization, is a good, positive way to get past certain feelings like anger and resentment.

Assertiveness: The Short Version

You can find entire books on the subject of assertiveness, but for our purposes, we're going to boil down the subject to a quick, three-step strategy that will keep you from becoming a doormat:

1. Begin with the words *I feel.* "*I feel* like you're using me as a punching bag." "*I feel* passed over for other people."

2. Move on to the words *I want.* "*I want* to be treated with respect and consideration." "*I want* to be noticed and acknowledged just like the others are."

3. End with the words *I will.* "*I will* let you know when I think I'm being treated disrespectfully and *I will* expect you to own up to it." "*I will* be asking you for regular reviews so that I can have an ongoing assessment of my performance."

This simple, three-step process can go a long way toward getting you out of a pattern that doesn't feel right.

I grew up in a very quiet, polite family in rural Minnesota. When I got to New York, I wasn't prepared for how aggressive big-city people can be. I had to learn all about assertiveness training, but hey, it's not rocket science. One point that stuck out for me was that being assertive and being aggressive are two entirely different things. It's important to be assertive— to not allow people to walk over you—but being assertive doesn't mean that you can't be the same nice, gentle, kind person you've always been. Being assertive actually makes life easier for you and for the people you work with.

Conflict Resolution

There isn't a team in the world that doesn't have its share of conflicts. The way to manage conflict, both on the job and off, is through *conflict resolution*. Without conflict resolution—which we can define as "the means by which to negotiate differences and come to some form of mutual agreement"—the tensions and bad feelings that can develop may linger to produce even deeper rifts. Your colleagues said the following about conflict resolution:

I'm the controller of a hotel and conference center in Denver, and I have a bunch of people on my team— the assistant controller, the general cashier, the night audit manager, and various personnel in accounts receivable and accounts payable. As the department head, part of my job is to manage my team, and one thing I've really chosen to concentrate on is conflict resolution. Generally, we're a pretty even-keeled group, but we have our occasional problems. The thing that I always stress about conflict is that it's a two-way street, so you have to ask yourself what part *you're* playing. Passive people contribute to conflicts just as much as aggressive people do—maybe even more. You have to study your behavior and own up to your part.

👑 What is your response to conflict? Ask yourself that question. Do you become super-sensitive? Does a harsh word cause you to become highly emotional? Do you respond to anger by evoking guilt or playing people against each other? Are you unyielding, and do you insist on always being right? How comfortable are you with anger altogether?

👑 If you ask me, the single most important factor in assuring successful conflict resolution is commitment. Everybody involved has to be committed to getting beyond the problem.

👑 You know the old joke about the husband and wife who start reminiscing about anniversaries past and when they remember a whopper of an argument they had on their fifth, it all comes back to them, fresh as bread from the oven, and they fight all over again? Well, like a lot of old jokes, there's plenty of truth in it. Always treat each conflict as a totally discrete, stand-alone situation. Don't look back, and don't reconstruct old conflicts. When you start saying things like "What about that time I filled in for you, and you never even bothered to say thank you?" then you can immediately wind up in the middle of an old fight. Don't go there!

👑 Hey—you're not a boxer. You don't have to worry about "winning" a fight. Never think in terms of "winners" and "losers" when it comes to conflicts. Think instead of conflict as a problem that two people share. That's the operative word: *share.* Turn to the person you're having the conflict with and say, "Frank, let's you and I figure a way out of this mess, okay?" Enlist the other person. Make it collaborative. Now *that's* winning.

👑 Here's a good trick to have up your sleeve: when you're trying to find your way out of a conflict, try using the name of the person you're having the conflict with. "Okay, Phyllis, I can see you're upset." "Stan, let's find a time to talk about this." "Geri, why do you think we seem to be having problems with each other lately?" The use of the other person's name signifies that you see him or her as a *person*, not as an enemy, and that will go a long way toward patching things up.

👑 Turning the other cheek can be a very good strategy in a situation of anger. Try just walking away from somebody who's having a meltdown, and you'll see how right that can feel.

👑 Never underestimate the power of an apology . . . preferably one with flowers. Even if you think the other person is wrong, apologizing will often work to your benefit. Not only might you engage the goodwill of the person you're having the conflict with, but you'll also look like a real mensch in the eyes of the rest of your coworkers.

Anger Management

All of us need to continually work at refining our conflict resolution skills, but a lot of conflict can be avoided if we can simply learn to better manage our anger. Remember, while anger in and of itself is not necessarily destructive, we all have different anger "styles," and any of these styles can become destructive if they are allowed to go unchecked. The most visible and disturbing anger style is the notoriously explosive road rage variety, which often ends in a violent outcome. Other people may have passive or passive-aggressive styles of anger. They don't seem to "do" anything, but they can inspire huge amounts of anger by "acting out" in ways such as being late, forgetting responsibilities, breaking important equipment, and so on. People with these anger styles are tough to deal with, because they're usually masters of denial. What is your anger style, and how well do you manage your anger? Your colleagues speak out on this issue.

When I was growing up, my father was an alcoholic, and he would go into terrible rages. It left me terrified of anger, even into my adulthood. After a lot of psychotherapy, I have come to recognize that anger is a perfectly normal part of life. Now, instead of suppressing my anger, I can "take my temperature" in a charged situation and ask myself, "Am I annoyed? Irritated? Really upset? In a rage?"

✧ I don't have a big problem with anger, but I do find that being in situations of anger can sap me of my energy, so I try my best to avoid such situations. I work with certain people who are—how shall I say it? A tad peculiar? I try to avoid confrontations with them. I don't "move their cheese," if you know what I mean. I stay out of their way. It's not a question of cowardice, believe me. It's a question of non-engagement and preserving my energy for better things.

✧ Mom always used to tell me to count to 10 when I was angry (and to chew my food 100 times and sit up straight). I thought it was corny when I was younger, but now I know that she was right. Counting to 10 really does help. It breaks the pattern. So does deep breathing. So does going for a walk. Whatever works . . .

✧ There are certain red-flag words that will immediately up the ante on a quarrel. Words like "never" (You *never* do what I ask you to do) and "always" (You're *always* forgetting things). Those words are like paper cuts. They hurt.

✧ Remember this: whatever you say, cannot go unsaid. It will always be there, in the mix.

✧ The most, most, most important thing is to *never* leave a paper trail. We're all so used to using e-mail now that when we're arguing with someone, we might have a tendency to sit down at the computer, jot off a blistering e-mail, and then push send. Well, once you push that button, you can never take back what you've written in the heat of anger. So don't do it!

Feedback and Criticism

To function effectively on a team, you need to be able to give and receive criticism and feedback. Even when feedback is couched in supportive terms, it can still be difficult for many of us to accept it with good feelings. We must get beyond this attitude, however, for if we are unable to receive constructive criticism, then we will find it difficult to grow. Let's hear what some of your fellow hotel and motel professionals have to say on the subject.

♛ I'm the food and beverage manager for a hotel in Vermont, and, as I see it, a big part of my job is to give my staff feedback and criticism. I just wish people were better at hearing me. Some of them are so thin skinned. Like I'll say, "Reggie, we need to pick up the pace on receiving these deliveries," and Reggie will be in a funk for two days. Maybe I'm doing something wrong . . .

♛ I think a large part of how you handle criticism is how you were given it as a child. My parents, thank goodness, were very reinforcing. They would always say things like, "Marcia, you've done a beautiful job at making your bed, but next time you might want to try doing it this way." Well, the fact is I was eight years old and I did a rotten job of making my bed, but they knew I was trying. My best friend Rachel had parents who would say things like, "Look how you make your bed! You're such a slob! You can't do anything right!" In other words, abuse, and so Rachel has never had an easy time accepting criticism . . . or staying in a job for very long.

🔱 For me, criticism has to be honest and direct. I'm a lounge manager, and one of my bartenders is this really cute, good-looking, upbeat guy who's late all the time. So I was really honest with him. I said, "Jim, if you're late one more time this week, we'll have to call it quits. I like the quality you bring to the job, but the anxiety of not knowing whether you'll show up when the bell rings is too much for me." Jim heard me—I couldn't have been more honest and direct—and he's changed his habits. Now that's a good resolution, as far as I'm concerned.

🔱 Never criticize people for things they can't change. If someone is a slow learner, don't criticize him for not being a quick study. If someone is awkward, don't criticize him for being clumsy. Find ways to reinforce their good points.

🔱 Managers have to learn how to give good feedback. I was the assistant manager of a motel in Oklahoma when I was just a kid—21 years old—and I was so invested in being everyone's best friend and never insulting anyone, particularly anyone older than me, that I was kind of spinning my wheels. Finally, one of the housekeepers—an older woman named Jan—came to me and said, "Fred, are you ever going to tell me how I'm *really* doing?" That made me realize that I wasn't doing anyone a favor by being so nice. My staff didn't need smiles and hugs, although there's nothing wrong with those. What they really needed was some honest assessment of their performance. That's an employee's right.

Gender Issues

Gender issues used to be hidden away, but not in the twenty-first century. As a professional in the hotel and motel world, you need to know how to handle issues of gender that may arise.

Women in Power

Many cultural myths and unwritten rules affect the way men—and women—feel about women in power. Powerful women often are seen as overly ambitious, manipulative, and power hungry, whereas men in power are seen in much more positive terms, such as strong, decisive, and highly attractive. We spoke to our hotel and motel professionals to see how they've been dealing with this issue.

👑 I work as a front desk supervisor in a hotel in Orlando. I never worked for a woman before I came here, and found myself reporting to Stella, our resident manager. I come from kind of a macho family, and I had my doubts. Stella is quiet, ladylike, and I guess I expected her to be a weak leader. But guess what?

She's not! She's very strong, very detail oriented, very centered, *and* she's kind and compassionate. I think I love women bosses!

👑 I'm a banquet manager for a hotel in Niagara Falls, and I'm a woman. I come from a family where I was the only girl—I had four brothers—and I guess that was good training for the hotel world. All I know is that I don't have a problem giving orders and holding my own. Frankly, I think assertiveness is a problem for a lot of women in positions of power, but the good news is that anyone can learn how.

👑 I have a woman boss, and I like her, but she's a little uptight. I wonder if women feel as loose in work situations as men do? Maybe they're overcompensating, or whatever. The male bosses I've had joke around more, take us out for a beer—you know what I'm talking about. My woman boss—it's a little like she's learning a foreign language, you know? Power doesn't come so naturally to her.

Sexual Harassment

Nothing will disrupt the team feeling as quickly as sex in the workplace, particularly sexual harassment. What is it exactly, and what do you do about it? Your colleagues comment.

👑 You'll know it when it's happening. Your boss will start saying things like, "You look great today, Wendy. New lipstick?" And then, a week later, it'll be, "You really know how to wear that dress, kid." And then it'll be, "Got the second skin on today, huh, honey?"

Rule of thumb: if a compliment doesn't *feel* like a compliment, then it's not a compliment. Comments about your hair, your clothes, your shoes, your fingernails do not belong in the workplace!

👑 Harassment takes on a life of its own. It usually comes from very compulsive people who engage in it all the time. Don't expect your harasser to stop on his own. He'll stop when you let him know that you have zero-tolerance for what he's doing.

👑 I was harassed when I was young and working at a motel in Memphis. My manager, I later learned, was famous for it. When it first happened, I felt absolutely violated, but my aunt, who'd had the same kind of experience at her workplace, told me how to handle it, and I still think it's great advice. She told me to rehearse a speech. Not to get all upset and stuff, because often that will just fuel these creeps, who get off on it. Very calmly and smoothly (or as smooth and calm as you can manage to be under the circumstances), you say something like this: "What you just said to me is offensive, and it upsets me very much. In fact, you're making it impossible for me to do my job under these circumstances. Would you want someone to say these things to your mother or your daughter or your sister? I bet you wouldn't. So just stop saying them to me." Well, he got the point—fast—and I never had to say another word.

👑 If you tell someone to stop harassing you, you need to follow it up with a written note restating your request within no more than 24 hours of the offense.

The note can be delivered to the person's desk or workstation, or it can be sent by registered letter to the office or his home. You should also send a copy to your human resources department.

🔱 Keep a written account of whatever is said or done to you. It will be evidence down the road if you need it.

🔱 Never put yourself in a vulnerable position. Don't be naïve. Think and act defensively. If you've got uneasy vibes about somebody, don't go out to lunch, just the two of you. Don't come in early or stay late if that means you're going to be alone with that person. This goes for whether you're the person being harassed or whether you're the person who might be unfairly accused of harassing.

🔱 If you've been harassed, there are probably other people at work who have been harassed too. People who harass are not that picky; they're usually serial offenders. Ask around very carefully—you don't want to slander anyone—to see if there's a trend going on.

🔱 Report harassment *immediately* to your supervisor. If your supervisor *is* the harasser, and there's nowhere higher to go, talk to an attorney.

🔱 The sad fact is that if you're being harassed, you may have to quit your job. Whether you will wind up getting any legal satisfaction or not is a whole other story. The main thing though is not to allow yourself to be victimized. Nothing is worth that. There are other jobs out there. Start looking now.

✇ Research the issue of sexual harassment on your own. A good place to begin is the Web site of the U.S. Equal Employment Opportunity Commission at <http://www.eeoc.gov>.

The Diverse Workplace

Few work worlds are as culturally diverse as the hotel and motel field. A lot of the entry-level positions in the field, such as housekeepers and dishwashers, for instance, attract new immigrants. The high end (i.e., general managers) also attracts an international contingent, such as people who have been trained in the famous Swiss hotel schools. If you're working in a big city, expect to be working alongside men and women from the European Union, Asia, South and Central America, and Africa. This diversity can be very stimulating, but it can also be something of a challenge to navigate. Some pointers follow:

✇ I'm from Spain, and I work at a hotel in San Diego, and I think the United States is super-duper, but people here should remember that other places in the world matter just as much.

✇ Each culture comes with its own set of values and attitudes. As Americans, we may think that people who don't look us in the eye when we talk to them are shifty or have something to hide. But in other cultures, there is much more of a sense of deference between superiors and subordinates, and the subordinate party will never look directly at the superior party. You have to know and remember things like that when you deal with people from diverse backgrounds.

✥ Part of what we do to build a team around here is that we don't make jokes about anybody from any ethnic group. It's not allowed. Simple as that. Those jokes reinforce offensive stereotypes.

✥ Here's something worth remembering: People who are not native English speakers are not deaf. You do not have to speak to them *in a very loud voice*.

We could go on and on about team building, but now we'd like to proceed to our next subject: customer service.

Chapter 5

Service with a Smile

Okay, be honest. Did the title of this chapter turn you off? Such a cliché, you claim.

The fact is, "service with a smile"—like most clichés—has a real nugget of truth in it. There will be much for you to learn from this chapter, but if nothing else, you'll come to realize that a smile and a warm, approachable attitude are not only recommended but *required* in the hotel and motel business. To offer anything less is falling down on the job. It's as simple as that.

To understand our point, all you really have to do is recall the many ways in which you yourself have been disappointed as a customer. The fact is, no matter how involved we may be in serving others, we all find ourselves the servee instead of the server at one time or another. We asked our hotel and motel professionals to recall their own nightmares regarding poor service, and their replies follow:

👑 What really puts me over the edge? When I pull away from the drive-in window at the donut shop and once I get back on the road I find out that the coffee I ordered "light and sweet" is black. I mean, how could I have been any clearer?

👑 I think it was that time I checked into a motel in Cleveland for this convention and I discovered that the reservationist—or should I say "the so-called" reservationist—had neglected to note that I requested a nonsmoking room. Her mistake meant a sleepless night for me.

👑 What kills me? When I call a hotel to make a reservation and I'm put on hold . . . and hold . . . and hold, all the time listening to "Jingle Bells" in February.

Do any of the above scenarios sound familiar? Can you feel your blood pressure rising just thinking about such events? Too often we find ourselves at the mercy of so-called "service people" who couldn't care less. This chapter will provide an overview of service—what constitutes good service, what makes service bad, how you can personally improve your service delivery, and how you can motivate your staff to do the same. Let's begin with the guests to try to get an idea of what they're looking for.

Wilkommen, Bienvenue, Welcome . . .

When you consider your guests, the best place to start is to think about the circumstances under which they are coming to your establishment. Some of the following may apply:

Your guest is

- traveling for business and is tired and pressured.
- traveling for pleasure and is excited and full of expectations.
- visiting from out of town for a special occasion—a wedding, a bar mitzvah, a reunion, or perhaps a sad event, such as a funeral.
- enjoying a romantic getaway.
- en route to a new home.
- recently retired and is on a long, cross-country trip.
- staying with you while his or her spouse or child is undergoing medical treatment at a nearby hospital.

In the hotel and motel field, you are dealing with people whose day-to-day experiences are heightened for one reason or another. Their fatigue level, thirst for adventure, or romantic inclinations may be higher than usual. In any case, it's not just the "same old, same old" for them. At least for the moment, they have raised the bar on their life experience. Your job is to figure out what they're looking for and what *you* need to do to satisfy them.

Figuring this out is part art, part science, and the practice of this discipline has been given a name: guestology. This word, coined by the Walt Disney Company—perhaps one of the world's best-run organizations—is two-pronged. On the one hand, guestology embraces *demographics*, the scientific study of who your guests are. Where do they come from? How did they reach you? Do they have any special needs? Are they traveling with children? Guestology also takes into account *psychographics*, which explores how the minds of guests work. What are your guests looking for on this trip? What excites them? What turns them off? When it comes to customer service, the credo of the Disney Corporation is to *exceed guests' expectations* and to *pay attention to detail.* That is why when you visit a Disney theme park, you are unlikely to walk away with coffee that is black when you've ordered it with cream and sugar.

With the idea of guestology in mind, we asked your colleagues in the hotel and motel industry their opinions regarding the primary needs and desires of their guests.

👑 Guests are looking for the smile. Whether it's from the front-line staff, the bell captain, or the hostess in the lounge, they want to know that people care about them, and nothing conveys that faster than a smile. And you know what? You don't even have to *see* a smile. You can *hear* a smile when you call up to book a room and the person on the other end has some real human warmth.

🕸 Guests want to feel safe—first and foremost. They're in a strange place, and that may make them feel a little uneasy. They want to know that they are safe from harm and that their belongings are safe. Remember too that safety and cleanliness go hand in hand for most people.

🕸 Using a person's name is a surefire way to make them feel good. "Hello, Mr. Phillips. It's so nice to have you with us." "Yes, Mrs. Lawrence. Of course we can get you a cab."

🕸 Guests are always looking for signals that they're getting real service. They want to feel like their experience is different from what they would get at home. That's why the proverbial chocolate on the pillow is so powerful. Your spouse is not going to put a chocolate on your pillow!

🕸 Anticipating your guests' needs is even more powerful than meeting their needs. If your guest inquires about a movie or a show, ask if he'd like a recommendation for a restaurant as well. If she's going out for a run, point out a popular route. If your guests have cameras around their necks, tell them about the amazing Ansel Adams exhibit at the museum. Always try to stay one step ahead of your guests. They'll love you for it.

🕸 There's a formula that everyone in this business should know about. It's called the "value equation."

It looks like this:

$$\frac{\text{Whatever the customer got}}{\text{Whatever it cost the customer}} = \text{Value}$$

Food for thought, no?

🐝 Your guests are often people in a strange city who need information. It's not enough to just hand them the Yellow Pages and say, "Go!" The staff needs to know about transportation, restaurants, local sights, weather, and so forth. That's part of the job.

🐝 Service is usually associated with the speed of delivery. Guests don't want to wait for things, and why should they? Haven't you ever been a guest at one of the so-called "better" hotels and had the experience of waiting a half an hour for room service to show up, or calling down to the desk for more towels and then sitting there trying to imagine what could possibly be taking so long? Waiting for things that should be done quickly and crisply translates into two words: service failure.

🐝 Don't feel that you have to run around your guests like circus dogs doing tricks. The best kind of service may not even register consciously on your guests. It is simply *there*—quiet and unobtrusive. Most guests only really become aware of service when it breaks down and it *isn't* there.

🐝 Keep in mind that service failures *will* be publicized. Something about human nature dictates that people seem more eager to talk about failures than

Tips for Good Customer Service

Basically, to become good at customer service, you should develop the following:

🔖 *The fundamentals.* These are the basic skills—reading, writing, and math—that are necessary in order to execute the routines and tasks of your job and interface effectively with the public. Don't forget the fundamentals of listening and speaking too, as discussed in the previous chapter.

🔖 *The look.* To convey a professional demeanor, you'll need to maintain a certain appearance. If you wear a uniform, it has to be clean and pressed, with no rips, tears, or stains and no missing buttons. Shoes should be clean and polished and, if necessary, should match your outfit. It will be up to individual establishments to determine hair lengths and styles, jewelry preferences, policies on beards and facial hair, and other grooming standards.

🔖 *Sharp thinking.* When interfacing with the public, you'll need to be a problem solver. Developing your creative thinking skills also will come in handy. You need to think critically to make rational decisions.

🔖 *Being your personal best.* You'll want to embody the values that we universally acknowledge as positive ones: a sense of responsibility, consideration, kindness, self-motivation, integrity, and honesty.

Do you have to be a perfect human being to make it in this field? Hardly. There is no such thing. Just strive to be the best you can be.

successes. Think about it. Your friend has just been away on a trip. She glosses over the really good places she stayed—"Oh, they were lovely"—but she absolutely relishes telling you the horror story of the mouse in the room or the broken air conditioning. A bad service encounter will translate into bad press, which will, in turn, translate into lost booking opportunities down the road.

👑 People say that first impressions count, and they certainly do. But don't forget those last impressions. I think they're even more important. We've instituted this policy at our hotel in Winston-Salem where we give everybody a little "going away" present. It's just a token, really, and it's often seasonal. For instance, we'll give a departing guest a daffodil in the spring. In the winter, we'll say good-bye with a peppermint stick. It's just a little nothing . . . but it becomes a little something because it sticks in people's minds.

It Starts with an "A"

We're talking about *attitude*, which is really the heart of customer service. We alluded to it with our emphasis on the smile, but it's such an important issue that we'd like to expand on it a bit. Let's hear what others in the field have to say about the all-important attitude.

👑 To me, the basis for having a good attitude toward your guests is to have a good attitude about your work in general. I'm a reservations agent for a hotel in San

Francisco, and I don't have a problem feeling good about what I do. I like the people I work with. I love the hotel, which is a small, restored limestone mansion that is elegant and beautifully run in every respect. I adore San Francisco. I grew up in Topeka, Kansas, and for me, to be in a place with hills by the water . . . well, need I say more? Therefore, because I'm very happy with my situation, it's easy for me to maintain a good attitude toward my guests. That's pretty simple and straightforward, but it's the truth.

👑 A good attitude will really pay off—you'll see. I'm a concierge at a hotel in Boston, and I like to think of myself as being a very friendly, nice person. I enjoy people, and I like to show it. Well, a few weeks ago, I sent this sweet older couple off to this gallery show that was all about model railroads, because somehow, when I was talking to them, it came out that the husband was a model railroad buff. They were all excited, but when they trooped over there, they found out that the gallery had closed up shop! It must have all happened in a wink, because the flyer I had about the show was only a month old, and I didn't double check before I sent them. In other words, it was a boo-boo on my part, and this couple had every reason to be annoyed with me, but because I had made a friendly connection with them—because I had a good attitude where they were concerned—they took it in stride.

👑 Have you talked about the smile? I can't emphasize it enough. Smiling pays off—big time. I remember once when I was a front desk manager at this hotel in Austin and I had a young woman working for me who rarely cracked a smile. Once I suggested that she try it, and she said, "But I don't *feel* like smiling." So I said, "Look, Sandra. I don't feel like coming to work every day, but I do. That's the job—and smiling is a part of that job." Well, fortunately, Sandra went off to pursue her dream, she became a securities broker, and I replaced her with Nadja, who smiled all the time and made everyone happy.

🐝 Just because you smile, don't expect that you're always going to get a smile in return. Some people are just grumps. But don't take it personally. Don't let another person's grumpiness cause you to question your own basic friendliness and warmth.

🐝 When you talk about attitude, I think it's only fair to look at it in the context of the overall environment of your workplace. I've worked in some real hellholes, let me tell you. Places where if you had to take a day off to take care of a sick kid, you were treated like Public Enemy #1. It's pretty hard to maintain a cheerful, sunny attitude when people are treating you that way.

🐝 Want to know what I think constitutes one of the worst displays of bad attitude? When a guest is at the front desk, waiting to be helped, and the two clerks on duty are talking to each other about everything but what they're supposed to be paying attention to. Has that ever happened to you?

🐝 Being friendly is a great way to telegraph a good attitude, but by the same token, being overly friendly can turn guests off. When a guest wishes to engage in conversation, you'll know it. Until you do, keep your dialogue short and sweet. If you have a guest checking in who's from Tacoma, Washington, and you have a great aunt in Tacoma, Washington, but you haven't seen her in over 10 years, well, that's more than your guest wants or needs to know.

🤴 Use the right words and the right expressions for the tasks you perform. If you hand someone a room key, don't say, "There you go." Say, "Thank-you for staying with us, and please let me know if there is anything you require." Similarly, if someone says to you, "Thank-you for that information," don't say, "Uh-huh" or "Yeah." Say, "You're welcome." That's the way it's done. It's called "manners."

🤴 Steer clear of trade jargon. As a manager, I routinely call up my reservations people incognito to hear what they sound like. The other day, when one of my agents answered, she said, "How would you like your room configured?" So I said, "Flora, it's me—Frank. What is this 'configured' nonsense? I mean, how do you expect anyone on the outside to have a clue what you're talking about?"

🤴 Take your time. Don't rush the guests. Usually your urge to rush will barely save you any time at all anyway. It's like those drivers who tailgate and then pass you where they shouldn't, and when you catch up with them a few moments later at a red light, you have to ask yourself, "How much time did that person actually save?"

🤴 Put your paperwork on hold when a guest is in your presence. Paperwork can wait; guests cannot . . . or at least should not have to.

Guest Conflicts

We spoke about conflict resolution in the last chapter, but we'd like to revisit the subject here. Why? Because when service is not effectively delivered and expectations are not met, a sense of frustration can quickly develop on the part of the disappointed guest, and this can lead to conflict. Depending on the degree of anger management the guest can call upon, the conflict can spiral out of control. The classic example of this is the notorious airport scenario, where the customer is so dissatisfied by the service he or she is *not* getting that he or she essentially goes into a rage. Some pointers from your colleagues follow regarding the best ways to handle conflicts:

👑 The guest is always right. The guest is always right. I said—*the guest is always right!* Now we know that's not the literal truth. When a guest says, "Last time I was here you floated rose petals in the toilet bowl," you know she's thinking of another hotel. But at the very least, we have to act as if she's right. That's just the way it is. That's what comes with buying service.

👑 Most guests who complain are simply looking for solutions. If they call down to the desk to report that their air conditioner isn't working, they're not going to hold it against you if you can get the unit fixed or replaced real fast. They just want it done.

👑 Before you even start with the idea of conflict resolution, you'll have to ask yourself how you feel about criticism. Let's say a guest comes down in the morning and says, "I didn't get my wake-up call, and now I'm late for my meeting." If you're the sort of person who regards any kind of criticism as complaining and, by extension, as a personal attack on you, then you're not even going to be able to hear the rest of what your guest has to say.

👑 Always start with listening. Don't rush in with words of protest and self-defense. Hear what your guest has to say first. Look your guest in the eye to let him know that you're engaged in a real communication with him. Don't cross your arms. This is a defensive posture that inhibits dialogue.

👑 Start with the presumption that nobody's perfect, and your guests don't expect perfection. What they expect is for you to do your best when it comes to fixing what goes wrong.

👑 Excuses will get you nowhere. "I'm sorry, but I'm very overloaded because one of our staff has just gone into the hospital . . ." is *your* problem, not the guest's. The guest is paying good money, and it's not her job to worry about the infrastructure of your organization. Instead of excuses, you'll want to take action to resolve the problem. That usually means immediate follow-up to correct what went wrong, and a peace offering of some sort—a free breakfast coupon, let's say—to soothe any hurt feelings.

♛ Some people are just boors. They'll snap at you like you're the "hired help"—*Hand me my room key. Wake me at six. Get me some towels.* Don't let other people's rude behavior diminish you. Their insensitivity should not be a reflection on you. It's a reflection on them. Remember that.

♛ Keep a record of all conflicts, and note, in a narrative way, what happened and how they were resolved. This can become a standard text for your establishment that others can learn from.

Handling Diversity

One of the reasons you entered the hotel and motel industry is because you probably find the idea of diversity stimulating and enriching. We've found that many people who enter this field come from small-town backgrounds and really enjoy the interaction with an international clientele. Travel is, at its heart, a wonderful experience of exchange, and when you work in a hotel or other lodging situation, one of the best aspects of your job is that you meet *all kinds of people.* Let's hear what your fellow professionals have to say on this topic.

♛ It's really fantastic. As a concierge in Chicago, I deal with guests from all over the world, and I learn so much. Languages, styles of dress, modes of behavior—it's so eye-opening.

There's a Right Way and a Wrong Way . . .

Hotel and motel professionals need to educate themselves about worthwhile exchanges of dialogue that they can draw upon in a wide variety of conflict situations. Things that are not particularly useful to say—"I'll have to check with my manager and get back to you"—tend to keep the conflict in a holding pattern. Guests prefer to hear active, decisive responses from staff members rather than the predictable passing of the buck. So the following are some good responses for your repertoire:

Wrong Way	Right Way
"That's not my job."	"Let me find the right person for you to talk to."
"That's impossible."	"I don't know the answer to that, but let me look into it and I'll get back to you by noon."
"Hey, I'm doing my best."	"I absolutely want to do the best I can for you. Please let me check into this."
"No one's ever complained about that before."	"It's an unusual request, but I'll check into it."

Some good things to say when people complain include:

- "Thank you so much for letting us know about this."
- "I totally understand. I'd feel exactly the way you do."
- "I'm so sorry. I'll take care of that immediately."

And, best of all:

- "I apologize."

👑 We had a situation in our hotel in Baltimore where we had a family from Nigeria staying with us while their son was being treated at Johns Hopkins University Hospital. They needed help with some language issues, and I found a translator for them through some contacts in Washington. I really got to know these people and, years later, I went to visit them in Nigeria. I'm still in touch with them.

👑 When we had the Olympics here in Atlanta, we had people staying with us from all over the globe. It felt like the UN around here.

So then, if the stimulus of dealing with international guests is one of the "perks" of working in the hotel and motel industry, what exactly are the best methods for making your guests feel comfortable in your establishment? Some pointers from colleagues follow:

👑 Okay, you've got a foreign guest and nobody can understand what he's saying. He's getting more and more agitated. (It seems that he's lost some money.) So what to do? The answer to that problem is to deal with things *before* they become a problem, not after. In other words, go through your entire staff and compile a list of anyone who has any multilingual capacity. You may have a housekeeper who speaks Portuguese. You might have an engineer who speaks Japanese. Your sous chef could be fluent in German. You may not have any idea what your resources are until you start looking into it. Once you have an idea, you need to create an in-house directory that you can draw upon as the situation calls for.

🪭 I manage a small hotel in Des Moines, and obviously we are not a hub for international visitors. Even so, we get our share. What we do is we maintain a list of Internet sites where we can get translations for most languages. We also keep a bare-bones list of Q's & A's in most of the main languages—Spanish, French, German, Italian, Portuguese, Chinese, Japanese, and so on—to deal with the basic questions and issues that come up. "How much is . . . (a room, breakfast, etc.?)," or "Where do I find a . . . (bank, taxi, bar, etc.?)."

🪭 Watch your voice level. Often, when we try to communicate with someone who is not speaking our language, we're guilty of speaking much too loudly, as if sheer volume will get us over the hump. It doesn't, and in fact just winds up making everyone feel even more frustrated.

🪭 Don't forget to take subtle cultural differences into account. For instance, many Americans are demonstrative and like to touch people. Visitors from other countries, like Japan, however, are not accustomed to being touched by strangers and will not understand or appreciate it.

🏰 I started in this field as a bellhop at a hotel in Washington, D.C., and, with all the international visitors you get there, I had a lot to learn. Just picking up a stranger's bag, for instance, can become a very loaded exchange. Most Americans wouldn't think twice about having a bellhop pick up their bags, but some people from other countries may feel very threatened if you go to pick up their personal belongings.

🏰 Americans can be a more informal bunch than some of the visitors from other countries. So should you be more relaxed or more formal with guests? The answer, as far as I'm concerned, is more formal. You're not going to offend anyone by being a little formal. You can always warm up if you get the opportunity, but as a rule, formality is the way to start.

The Extra Touch

We stated at the beginning that one thing most guests look for when they travel is the feeling that they are truly being pampered. That's what makes travel feel different from staying at home. There are so many ways to make guests feel special, but the

Comment Cards

Comment cards can be an excellent way to gather data on guest satisfaction. Some pointers follow:

✦ Make sure the comment card has a sealing device, and ask your guests to provide their names, room numbers, and dates of stay.

✦ Place the cards in a prominent spot in every room.

✦ Offer an incentive for filling out a comment card. For example, "Fill out a card and get a free video rental."

✦ Place locked drop boxes for the cards at key locations.

✦ Review the comment cards with your staff in an organized, timely way. Creating a database with a spreadsheet or software that generates charts and graphs is a valuable way to share the information.

✦ Institute some sort of follow-up strategy with guests whose comment cards express dissatisfaction. An incentive for their return—"Free use of health club upon your revisit," for instance—may sway them.

following ideas from hotel and motel professionals are particularly memorable:

✦ I'm the manager of a boutique hotel in New Orleans. One of my staff came to me with an idea that

I thought was so cute and creative that we decided to go with it, and it's been a big hit. It's a "pillow menu." Upon check-in, or even before, by phone or e-mail, our guests get to choose what kind of pillow they prefer. Firm, soft, down, synthetic . . . we even have an anti-snoring pillow! Now that's something you're not going to get at home.

👑 We run a ski lodge in Stowe, Vermont, and what's the one thing our guests seem to love more than anything? The fact that they can raid the kitchen, on the house, from 10 to midnight any night of the week. We put out all kinds of nibbles—cheeses, cut-up veggies, cookies, mini-muffins—and they just go. Of course, it costs a bit of change, but in terms of customer loyalty, it's worth its weight in gold.

👑 We own a B&B in Quebec, and we're always on the lookout for new ideas. We go to home shows and find special little things that we can incorporate into our environment to make our guests feel even nicer. Things like polar fleece throws and chocolate spoons to stir the coffee or a putting green that can be easily set up in a guest's room.

👑 It's amazing what's out there in terms of raising the pampering bar. I'm a food and beverage director for a hotel in Las Vegas, and on my time off, what do I do? Check out the competition, of course. So recently I stayed at this incredible resort in Acapulco, and they had—get this—a bath menu! The bath butler comes in, and you get to choose if you want lime or rosemary or lavender or peppermint scents, and then he tosses petals in the water and sets up cognac if you want. Amazing!

🛏 Sometimes we'll get letters from guests who have stayed with us—we own a small inn in Williamstown, Massachusetts—and do you know the #1 thing everybody thanks us for? The hot water bottles in the rooms. People love them. They're old-fashioned and quaint . . . and really warm!

🛏 I'm a resident manager at a very trendy hotel in Vancouver. We get a lot of young, hip professionals, and instead of putting a chocolate on the pillow, we decided to put a condom there instead. We feel like we're doing our bit for safe sex, and the clientele appreciates our sensibility.

Guests with Special Needs

Your hotel may have its share of visitors with special needs. A policy should be put into place to deal with these situations *before* the fact, not afterward. A few things to keep in mind follow:

🛏 Seniors need good light by the bedside, in the bathroom, and in closets. They need radios and clocks whose numbers and dials can be easily read. Grips in the bathrooms are welcome, and an abrasive tub bottom is a must. So are banisters on all stairways. Put a night-light in the room, or at least in the bathroom. Seniors often need to get up to go to the bathroom during the night, and if you don't provide a night-light, then they'll leave the bathroom light on all night long, which will wind up costing you a lot more money in the long run. And don't forget—travel is one of the biggest priorities among seniors who have the time and often the disposable income to indulge in it. Don't bar

Avoid Hidden Charges

While a "little something extra" is often a welcome touch, a "little something extra that's hidden in your bill" is decidedly not. There are all sorts of small surcharges floating around, including:

- Exorbitant hotel and motel telephone and fax charges.
- Charges for in-room safes.
- Restocking fees for mini-bars.
- Service charges added on to room service charges.

Not all of these are objectionable in and of themselves, but guests should be made aware of them before being charged. Guests may certainly opt to spend a dollar a night to use an in-room safe, for instance, where they can store a laptop, but charging for an in-room safe that guests haven't used or may not even know about will probably alienate them. Generally, hidden charges create more lost revenues in terms of turned-off guests than they provide revenues in terms of added income.

this constituency from your prospective clientele by failing to meet their needs.

For guests with physical disabilities, three things should be kept in mind when booking their rooms: (1) Give guests rooms close to restaurants or food courts; (2) Make sure guests' rooms are easily accessible to the entrance or transportation; and (3) Alert staff members to go out of their way to accommodate the needs of guests with special needs.

We conclude this chapter on guest service with a point that everyone in the hotel and motel field should keep in mind. *Be a guest at your own lodging.* This is particularly important if you're in a managerial position. Go from check-in to checkout *as a guest.* Don't stay in the fanciest suite in the hotel either. Pick an average room, and then really examine it from a guest's perspective. Take a shower and a bath so you can experience the flow and availability of hot water. Did you have enough towels? Were they fluffy enough? Was it comfortable for you to read a book in bed? How was the light? How did the room smell? Was it warm enough? Too warm? Did the shades keep out the morning light? Could you hear noises coming from other rooms or from equipment? Did you book a reservation and eat in the restaurant? Was it a pleasurable experience?

The only way to really know if you're servicing your guests is to try to become one yourself. Unfortunately, you probably won't be able to pull off the incognito bit, but even so, a view from the inside provides a whole new slant on where you're succeeding and where you're falling down on the job.

Chapter 6

Taking Care of Yourself

*W*orking in the hotel and motel industry, you may often reach the point where you feel that *you* are the one who needs to be in a hotel. *You* are the one who deserves to be pampered, who longs to lie on a chaise with a pineapple-rum drink, who needs the seaweed wrap at the spa more than any of your guests do.

Guest envy is a real factor in this field, particularly when you're feeling overworked, overtired, and generally stressed out. The purpose of this chapter is to offer some helpful hints on how to identify the stress factors in your life, how to deal with them, and how to control them instead of having them control you.

To begin, the underlying premise of our discussion is that the real antidote to stress, in the broadest sense, is *wellness*. A well body, a well mind, and a well spirit give you a fighting chance at beating stress. Wellness, too, is closely connected to the concept of *wholeness*—the idea that human beings are organisms whose individual parts are all interconnected. The word *holistic*, with which you may be familiar, comes from the idea of "wholeness." A holistic outlook is based on the belief that the mind influences the workings of the body, and the body influences the workings of the mind.

To make the most of your energies and to aim for and achieve the success to which you're aspiring, you will need to learn how to pace yourself, how to deal with frustration and disappointment, and how to develop strategies that will protect you from exhaustion. After all, you're in this for the long haul . . . and at certain times in your career, it surely *will* feel like a long haul.

If we were only able to make one important point in this chapter, it would be that the key to wellness is to act *preventively* rather than *reactively*. In other words, dealing with a problem *after* the fact is far more complicated and difficult than dealing with it *before*. In this chapter, we'll be identifying the risks you face and the coping strategies that can help you skirt these risks. Let's start with the subject of food.

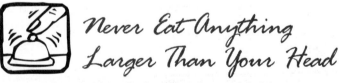

Never Eat Anything Larger Than Your Head

As a professional in the hotel and motel field, you may be having a tough time staying on top of what you eat. You'd like to think that you have the whole issue of food and nutrition squared away—after all, you watch your carbs and sugar intake, you go easy on the salt, you count your fat calories, and you monitor your caffeine and alcohol intake—but that's all *when you're at home.* When you're on the job—and you're on the job for long stretches at a time—you don't always have such control, and you may wind up eating and drinking things that you know are not the best for you.

Remember that plate of Buffalo chicken wings you ate at 11 P.M. the other night? How about that Black Forest cake that Chef Jean sent up for you? And did you really need your third Cosmopolitan at the cocktail party?

In our culture, we're surrounded by food rules and food abuse. Most of those rules can be taken, as it were, with a grain of salt. After all, when we ban certain foods—fats, carbohydrates, and such—we make them "forbidden fruits," and we can run into trouble that way. The idea of a balanced diet is one that is still worth thinking about, and that's why the one and only food rule we hold onto is: "Never eat anything larger than your head." That will always make good sense to us, whereas all of the other "food rules" are just ways of giving food more emphasis in our lives than it should really have.

Still, we live in a culture that has so many issues around food that few of us can manage to stay clear and neutral on the subject. Obesity is now right alongside smoking and drinking as a major public health problem. Eating disorders, such as anorexia and bulimia, are rampant, particularly among young women. We live in the richest society in history, but we have affluent teens who are literally starving themselves to death. We are so bombarded with food advertisements and food messages that the whole emphasis on food in our culture has gone out of whack. So how do you protect yourself from that? Let's hear what your colleagues have to say.

🐚 Working as a front desk clerk in a first-class hotel in Houston, I'm often on night shifts, and that means that I eat restaurant food a lot. So what's wrong with that picture, you may ask. After all, it's delicious, isn't it? Of course, it's delicious—too delicious! I overeat. I indulge in the dessert buffet. I do things that I would never do if I were eating at home. And, as a result, I'm putting on weight.

🐚 As director of marketing for a resort in New Mexico, I regard information gathering as an important aspect of my job. And, obviously, I wouldn't be in this field in the first place if I didn't love to travel. So I take vacations regularly, and when I do, I always set out for some part of the world I haven't been to before. What I've come to see is that very few parts of the world are as confused about food as we are. Seriously—spend time in the south of France or Italy or Spain, and you'll see that the Mediterranean culture is incredibly sane about food. People revere cheeses and breads and wines, but they don't use any of it to excess. They eat lots of fruits and vegetables and nuts and healthy oils. Japan is another place where people just seem to have a very sane relationship to food. But here in the United States, people go to restaurants where the portions are vulgar and enormous and everything is supersized. It's just crazy!

🦋 I'm Swiss—I work as a *sous*-chef at a hotel in Miami Beach—and when I first came to this country, I was really confused about all the dieting. We would have people come to the restaurant, and there would be so many special orders! No sugar, no salt, no fat. How can a person cook this way?

🦋 I'm the director of food and beverage at a hotel in Sacramento, and frankly it's been hard for me to keep up with the whole low-fat/no-fat thing. Basically I think a lot of that is a scam. You see people slurping these enormous low-fat frozen yogurt sundaes with the low-fat butterscotch sauce and the low-fat whipped cream and the low-fat cherry on top, and I mean, give me a break. Who do they think they're fooling?

🦋 If you want to get a handle on the whole food thing—and I don't mean a "love handle"—then a good place to begin is with an understanding of the physiology and the psychology of hunger. When people say, "I'm hungry," they're not always saying the same thing for the same reasons, because there are different kinds of hunger. There's stomach hunger—think of that as "real" hunger—when you haven't eaten for a long stretch, and you start getting those familiar feelings we call "hunger pains." Then there's mouth hunger, which is when you smell a hot dog at the ballpark or a slice of pepperoni pizza, and you just feel like you have to have it, whether you're "really" hungry or not. And then there's the hunger that's set off by emotional needs, like when you're anxious or depressed or empty and you want to "fill yourself up." Figuring out what kind of hungry you are at any given moment is a big help when it comes to controlling your eating. If you resolve only to eat when you are "stomach hungry," then you may begin to see some dramatic results right away.

I know I shouldn't laugh, but sometimes I have to. I'm the director of catering for a hotel in Philadelphia, and of course we do all sorts of functions, everything from conventions to weddings to publicity launches and what have you. Well, sometimes I'll be standing there watching people, and I just can't believe how fast they eat! They go through plates of food like a buzz saw through white pine. These folks are chowing down their vegetable lasagna and their beef tenderloin so fast that their brains don't even have a chance to catch up with their mouths, so they don't feel satisfied afterwards. (Good thing Dr. Heimlich invented his maneuver, too, because the way they eat is just plain dangerous!) Eating slowly is a great way to get your appetite under control. I had one of those mothers, bless her heart, who used to tell me to chew each bite of food 50 times before swallowing. You know what? Mom was right. Eating slowly is good for the digestion, plus it gives you a chance to satisfy yourself.

If you're a chronic overeater, there are ways to play tricks on yourself. For instance, eating an apple before you have a meal will go a long way toward curbing your appetite. Even drinking a glass of water before a meal will do the trick. It fills you up so you won't have to take in as many solids.

Gimme Water!

As you may remember from your high school health class, your body is made up of 60 to 70 percent water. The loss of that water—through sweating, excretion, and so forth—demands that it be replenished. If you neglect your water intake, you'll be opening yourself up to fatigue and much worse symptoms, especially dehydration. Proper hydration is all-important, follow these tips:

❧ The kidneys need water in order to function properly. If they do not function as they should, that will, in turn, affect liver function. The liver metabolizes fat into energy for the body. If the liver needs to do the work of the kidneys, then less fat will be metabolized and more will be stored in the body.

❧ Water is important for muscle stimulation. Drink before and after exercise.

❧ People of average weight should drink eight glasses of water a day, or approximately two quarts. More water is necessary depending on factors like increased exercise or hot, dry weather.

❧ Stay ahead of the hydrating game. Once you begin to dehydrate, you have to work overtime to catch up. That translates into stress for your body.

❧ Nothing takes the place of water. Juices and sodas add calories where none are necessary. Fancy flavored waters hit you in the pocketbook, when, in fact, nothing is more thirst-quenching than plain, unadorned H_2O. And other liquids, like teas and coffee, actually act as diuretics, pulling water *out* of the body.

Binging on Diets

Quick, name a multibillion-dollar industry that gets people to spend money without offering any really substantial results. Did you say "gambling"? Not a bad answer, but the one we were looking for is the diet industry.

The diet industry—which takes in revenues of some *$40 billion* a year—is under attack by government agencies for making claims that cannot be backed up. In fact, while the diet industry spreads the impression that once the weight comes off, it stays off, the reality is that *95 percent* of dieters regain the weight they've lost, and many dieters in fact wind up putting on even *more* weight. Now government agencies have begun to prohibit diet companies from misrepresenting the likelihood of customers maintaining weight loss. But dieting can be more than disappointing—it can be downright dangerous. Let's see what your colleagues have to say on this topic.

 Most diets are scams. Now you see it, now you don't, now you see more of it. That's all smoke and mirrors. The reality is that there's no magic bullet when it comes to losing weight. It's all about what you take in and what you burn up.

 How do you lose weight? By burning more calories than you eat. How do you burn calories? By moving around more. I work in accounts payable at a

hotel in St. Louis, and I sit around all day long. I've made it a point, over the last few months, to give over my lunch hour to a nice long walk. That's all it took for me to start losing weight. I eat pretty much the same as I always did—which was never excessive to start out with—but now, with the walking, I'm starting to see results.

🐾 I read somewhere that the average American woman burns 1,600 to 1,700 calories a day. One hundred years ago, that same average American woman was burning about 2,500 calories a day. Why? It's not so hard to figure it out. Instead of pulling up at the drive-through to get a bucket of wings for dinner, she was out plucking chickens and butchering them and cooking them, all of which used up precious calories. Plus she was out wringing the laundry and stoking the smokehouse and carrying the coal and what have you.

🐾 I'm a reservationist at a hotel in San Juan, and as far as I'm concerned, it's a great job. My mother and two of my aunts worked in housekeeping for this same hotel, and they think I'm royalty. But sometimes, I have to confess, I look at the housekeepers a little wistfully because at least they get to *move* all day long. Me, I'm sitting at a computer workstation eight hours a day. I can feel my hips and rear end starting to spread, and there's not much I can do about it with all that stationary sitting!

🐾 Over the last six months, I started to feel like I was putting on too much weight, so I got some great advice from one of my girlfriends here at the hotel who works as a nutritionist. She told me to keep a journal for at least two weeks of everything I eat. She told me that when it comes to losing weight, the bottom line is simply calories in versus calories out.

Body Image

What's the underlying problem that drives so many millions to dieting? The bizarre body image that the advertising industry promotes. The normal American is so far removed from the supermodels whose images bombard us that we can't even tell anymore what's normal. Consider the following remarks:

🔱 We all have our set point when it comes to weight. I'm meant to weigh 135 pounds, so no matter how much I diet, that's where I'm ultimately going to wind up. Genetics is genetics—there's not a lot of arguing with it. But that doesn't mean you can't be a really fit and toned 135 pounds. Even if you're built large or stocky, you can still have a strong, healthy, and attractive body.

🔱 I went to this workshop at a yoga center on body image, and they had us do this amazing thing. They asked us to write down the names of three people in history we most admired. Well, people wrote down Martin Luther King, Eleanor Roosevelt, Gandhi, Jesus, Mother Teresa. Nobody wrote down Kate Moss or Courtney Cox or anybody like them just because they were skinny.

In fact, she said, most of us don't gain weight from eating enormous amounts of food or from going on binges but from the little things we do—or should I say "shouldn't do"?—every day. The cream-filled donut at four o'clock when a banana would work much better as a pick-me-up, or the 900-calorie carrot muffin with the cream cheese frosting for breakfast instead of a bowl of bran cereal. The journal exposes all your little habits, and then it's up to you to cut them out.

👑 Did you know that the average American gains anywhere from 20 to 30 pounds between the ages of 30 and 50, and that's only from eating an extra five to 10 calories a day? That sounds kind of depressing, on the one hand, but if you look at it the other way, it's kind of encouraging, because it's pretty easy to cut out five to 10 or even 50 calories a day, isn't it?

👑 Hey, let's get serious here. Many people die every year in this country as a result of being on dangerous diets. Diets below 1,200 calories a day can damage the metabolism within a matter of weeks, and it can take months and sometimes even years to regain a healthy metabolism. Don't play Russian roulette with your body!

 Fitting in Fitness

Watching what you eat is obviously important when you're trying to keep your weight under control, but when you combine weight watching with a fitness program, a certain synergy develops, and before you know it, the pounds start to melt away.

Don't reserve exercise for weight loss purposes, however. Instead, make it a regular part of your life for now and always. When you do, you'll discover that regular exercise has the magical capacity to help us think more clearly, combat stress, and ward off depression. Finding the time for regular exercise in a busy schedule can be a challenge. Some good ideas follow from fellow hotel and motel professionals:

👑 When it comes to exercise, the worst mistake you can make is setting the bar too high at the beginning. You'll soon become discouraged, and you'll be inclined to throw in the towel. Remember that exercise is not a contest. Exercise is something good you do for yourself.

👑 A lot of people say, "Oh, I wish I could, but I can't. I just don't have the time." But when you ask them how much time they think is involved, they're usually way overboard. Three to five exercise sessions a week is all you really need, anywhere from a half-hour to an hour per session. Now that's manageable in even the busiest lives, don't you think?

👑 Exercise goes so much better and faster when it's fun, so select a workout that suits you and that makes you feel good. Some people are water babies, and they should do their aerobics in a pool. Some adults still love the thrill of group sports, so why not play soccer or rugby or whatever, as long as your body can handle it? Then there are the people who love the combination of music and movement, and for these folks aerobic dancing may be the answer. You just need to figure out what you like and then stay with it.

✿ Reality check, people: you don't have to join any fancy gym or hire your own personal trainer in order to get into shape. You can get your exercise anywhere and everywhere. I'm not just talking about running or walking outside, either on the street or maybe at the high school track, but also doing things like walking up steps instead of using the elevator. If it's at all possible, walking to work is golden, because then you're combining your exercise with your commuting time. Another good idea is when you go to the mall, instead of circling for 20 minutes looking for a parking spot that's close to the stores, park really far away and use those 20 minutes to get in a good walk. As you develop that kind of thinking, you'll discover that there are fitness opportunities all over the place.

✿ Always listen to your body. If you feel pain, stop what you're doing. If you're breathing too hard to be able to carry on a conversation, then you're pushing yourself too hard. And before you even start on a fitness program, do what they tell you: consult your doctor.

✿ I was never a real exercise person, I have to admit. I tried exercising with a Walkman™ and while I watched TV, but in the end, neither TV nor music did it for me. The thing that really turned it around was getting an exercise buddy. My friend Paula and I walk four times a week now. If one of us feels unmotivated, the other one does a guilt trip. And once we get going, we talk about everything under the sun, so the time just flies by. It's been a real solution for me.

Ah, Sweet Slumber . . .

You can work out regularly, eat wisely, avoid tobacco and alcohol, and take your vitamins, but if you don't get the sleep you need, then you're never going to achieve real wellness. Sleep is one of the most important factors in your overall health picture. Scientists don't really know why sleep is so necessary, they just know that it is. Some theories speculate that sleep is so important because it is during sleep that the body processes certain chemicals that have built up. Speculation aside, sleep is clearly a refuge from the stress that is epidemic in our society. It is the time when our bodies rest from the overstimulation we receive from TV, the Internet, and just being out in the world. Unfortunately, a great many of us have a hard time accessing that respite. Poor sleep is one of the main complaints that physicians hear about, and if it goes unaddressed, it can quickly take its toll.

Insufficient sleep can affect you in a variety of serious ways. Research shows that after as few as six days of reduced sleep—meaning anything less than four hours—the body's ability to metabolize carbohydrates can be diminished. What exactly does that signify? Well, for one thing, it means that if you're sleeping less than you should at the same time you're indulging in junk food—which you're liable to do if you're stressed out from sleeping less—then you will have less capacity to metabolize all of those chips, corn dogs, and doughnuts, and you'll be more likely to develop a weight problem.

Sleep deprivation is also a leading cause of all kinds of accidents, including household accidents, industrial accidents, and, of course, vehicular accidents. According to the National Highway Traffic Safety Administration, sleep deprivation can be linked to over 100,000 automobile accidents that occur every year. Astonishingly, research shows that driving while sleep deprived can be every bit as deadly as driving under the influence. If you still believe that sleep deprivation is not such a big deal, consider this. In a research experiment that subjected laboratory rats to less and less sleep, the rats died within two to four weeks. Sleep is not only a delicious part of life, it's also absolutely essential.

So, then, what exactly constitutes an adequate amount of sleep? The answer, as it so happens, is not exact. The "right" amount of sleep varies from person to person. Most of us sleep in one long stretch of six to eight hours, which, subject to one's age, sleeping conditions, and other factors, can either be interrupted or blissfully unbroken. Then there are those among us who choose to sleep for five or six hours at a stretch and may perhaps supplement this with an afternoon nap. Consider your own sleep habits. Is it hard for you to fall asleep? Do you often wake up? Do you feel tired much of the day? Let's hear what your fellow professionals in the hotel and motel industry have to say on this subject.

✥ As a front desk clerk, I sometimes work days and sometimes nights. For anyone whose schedule is erratic like that, it's easy to fall into bad habits, like drinking too much caffeine on those nights when you have to work.

✥ I'm not the world's best sleeper. My mom said my sleep problems started when I got colic as a baby. So knowing this about myself, I try to steer clear of any stimulants that can lead me astray. I avoid coffee, tea, chocolate, colas, and anything else that has any caffeine after four in the afternoon. I don't eat spicy, heavy foods before I go to sleep. (One slice of pepperoni pizza and I'm tossing and turning all night long.) I'm very disciplined about exercise and hate to miss a day, but I'd rather miss a day than a night's sleep. So if I haven't fit exercise into my day, I forego it, knowing that if I run or bike too late at night, I'll be up for hours.

✥ As far as I'm concerned, when it comes to sleep, the magic word is *routine.* I try to go to bed the same time every night. I lie there for no more than a half hour reading a book. Then I put on some New Age music and then I'm asleep. If I stick with this routine, I'm in great shape. If I deviate from it, I'll often have sleep problems, but then I'll work at getting back to the routine, and I'm usually okay in a few days.

✥ The idea of a nap—curling up in a sunny window seat with an afghan and a fat cat—is very appealing, but in fact naps don't make for great sleeping habits. They tend to get competitive with your real nighttime sleep. So if you do nap, keep it to no more than an hour.

🐾 Try not to lie in bed and watch TV before you go to sleep. It may seem relaxing, but you're actually being electronically stimulated by the TV. Heaven knows, most of us get enough electronic stimulation during the day, sitting at our computers and whatnot. It's better to limit your presleep activities to something like taking a warm bath or listening to Mozart or reading a good book.

🐾 When it comes to sleep, I find myself very susceptible to changes in the environment. A room that's too cold or too hot can have me tossing and turning, and the same goes for a room that's too noisy or too quiet. Like Goldilocks said, it has to be *just* right.

🐾 If you live in a noisy apartment, like I do—my upstairs neighbor walks back and forth all night long in high heels, for some reason—then you might have to try something special, like one of those "white noise" machines that play sounds of nature, or else use earplugs. There are some excellent, super-pliable earplugs on the market these days.

🐾 If you have trouble sleeping, you shouldn't turn on the lights to read or watch TV. It's better to stick with your normal light-dark schedule and just lie there in the dark, listening to music if you want. Given half a chance, sleep will come.

🐾 Check out sleeping pills if you have to. There are a lot of new ones on the market that are really good.

But you should never be on them unless you're under the care of a doctor, and in any case, you shouldn't be on them for more than four weeks at a time.

Bad Habits

Some bad habits we can live with—fingernail biting, gum cracking—and some really should be decisively eliminated from our lives. At the top of that list is anything that falls into the category of substance abuse. We have already discussed overeating as a substance abuse issue, but now we're talking about smoking, drinking, and drug use. The number of American lives that are lost each year to these bad habits is absolutely staggering.

For those working in the hotel and motel industry, the easy availability of alcoholic beverages can pose a particular problem. Working in a hotel, you're never far from a bar or lounge, and the temptation of these watering holes can be hard to resist, particularly if you're in the habit of using alcohol as a stress reliever. It's never too soon to start exploring how you relate to these addictive substances. A good way to begin is to listen to what your colleagues in the field have to say on the subject.

As a general manager of a hotel in Indianapolis, I have to admit that I'm more inclined to hire nonsmokers over smokers. I can't actively ask someone on an interview whether he or she smokes, but if I see obvi-ous signs that someone does—let's say, tobacco stains on the fingers or teeth or maybe just the reek of ciga-rette smoke on clothing—then I'll probably pass on that person. I just feel that he or she is not going to be as healthy as a nonsmoker and, somewhere down the line, we're going to wind up paying for his or her bad habits.

🐦 If you're in a job where you're interfacing with the public—in a hotel setting or a restaurant—you'll quickly become aware that you'll have to deal, on a day-to-day basis, with other people's substance abuse problems. I'm a resident manager at a resort in Sedona, Arizona, and I have 25 years of experi-ence in this field. At every stage of my career, in every job I've ever held, I've dealt with these issues. I started in the business as a bartender, and I had the issue of withholding drinks from people who had already had too much. After I got my degree in hotel management, and I found myself in another end of the business, I was still dealing with these issues, having to break up parties of college kids where they wrecked rooms and did other charming things like that. It's a big problem in this field—a big, ugly problem.

🐦 As a catering manager, I'd have to say that the best thing that's happened in my life lately was when our hotel instituted a no-smoking policy in the dining room. No more cigarettes snuffed out in the mashed potatoes!

Need Help Stopping Smoking?

By now, we should all be clear on one thing: smoking is rotten for your health. It can—and *does*—cause lung problems, heart problems, bowel and bladder problems, and, of course, all sorts of cancers. If you've never smoked, *don't start!* If you do smoke—*stop!* The good news is that half of all American smokers have been successful in their efforts to kick the habit, so there's no reason you can't do the same. Keep the following important points in mind:

❧ Smoking low-tar, low-nicotine cigarettes is not a solution. It is part of the problem. They just make you puff harder and longer.

❧ Clove cigarettes and smokeless tobacco are just as bad as regular cigarettes. Clove cigarettes, also known as "bidis," actually produce *three times* as much nicotine and carbon monoxide as regular cigarettes and *five times* as much tar. Smokeless tobacco—like plug, leaf, and snuff—is as addictive as cigarettes and is linked to cancer, increased heart rate and blood pressure, and dental problems like gingivitis, gum recession, and tooth loss. And just try kissing someone who uses smokeless tobacco!

❧ In order to stop smoking, first you need the motivation. Then you need help. Where do you get the help? Start with your doctor or dentist. If that's not convenient, check out the Web sites of organizations like the American Lung Association (<http://www.lungusa.org>), the American Heart Association (<http://www.americanheart.org>), or the American Cancer Society (<http://www. cancer.org>).

 Never underestimate how addictive tobacco is. Its addictive qualities are so powerful, in fact, that you may have to experiment to find out what works for you in terms of kicking the habit. Maybe it's gum, maybe it's the patch, maybe it's hypnosis or an American Cancer Society program—check them all out, and when you find what's right for you, do it!

Stressed Out

In the tentative U.S. economy at the beginning of the twenty-first century, a significant amount of stress is connected to most jobs. We live in an era of conglomerates, where the firm you're working for today can easily mutate into something entirely different tomorrow. The old-fashioned model of job security—working in a position for 25 years, receiving a gold watch upon retirement—feels quite remote today.

It can be argued that all eras have had significant stresses, and that's true. Historians could even argue that we have less stress in our lives now than our ancestors did. After all, advanced technology offers us more leisure time, and advanced medical techniques have eliminated many problems that were once common and life threatening. But we also have rapidly developing overpopulation and pollution, and we live with the horrifying knowledge that a push of a button could destroy cities and even civilizations. Therefore, many people in the world today experience life as being *increasingly* stressful.

In addition to the stress that can be present at work and in the world at large are the stressors that each of us must confront in our own lives. A death in the family, marital strife, financial reversals, and illness or injury can create tremendous stress. So the question becomes, what can we do to counter all of this unhealthy stress? And unhealthy it is, for when stress goes untreated, it can cause physical complications such as high blood pressure, headaches, gastritis, and acid reflux. Let's hear how your colleagues in the hotel and motel industry confront and combat stress.

👑 The first thing to do is to learn how to become more flexible. I was always a control freak—I'm the first to admit it—but even old dogs can learn new tricks. When my doctor said that my blood pressure was moving into the danger zone, and that if I didn't learn how to ease off I'd be in big trouble, I made myself become a different person. I told myself that I didn't have to be perfect, and neither did anyone working for me. We're all human beings and, by our very nature, imperfect beings.

✠ I'd say that about 60 percent of my stress over the years came about as a result of my not being able to say no. I habitually took on too much and wound up always walking around with incredible pressure. I actually went to a life coach who taught me how to say that very complicated word: no. *No. No. No.* See? I can say it now. "No, I'm sorry, I can't make that appointment. My daughter's baby shower is that day." "No, I'm sorry, but I can't stay late. I told you. I have a commitment." "No, I can't take on that assignment. I'm already covering for Sandra till she gets back to work." Without that two-letter word in your vocabulary, you're going to be almost defenseless against pressure and stress.

✠ Stress can come into your life like a tidal wave. It has the quality of heightening everything and making everything loom large and look worse. "If I don't get this report done, I'm going to be fired. If I get fired, I won't be able to pay the mortgage, and my family and I will be out on the street. We'll be homeless. We'll starve!" It's so easy to get swept away by stress. You can stop the wave with a simple device like "STOP THOUGHT." When you feel yourself getting carried away, just hold up a STOP sign in your brain, and halt the thought right in its tracks. It really works.

✠ Make sure that you treat stress as a medical problem. Why? Because it is. Talk to your physician and put a stress management plan into place. The longer stress goes untreated, the more damage it can do. You may need medication to help you get beyond the stress.

Coping Strategies

So what can you do to make yourself feel better when you're under a lot of stress? Some practical, everyday ways to deal with stress follow, courtesy of your colleagues:

 Deep breathing is the place to begin. It's free, it's easy, and anyone can do it anywhere, anytime. Start by inhaling deeply through your nose, filling up your lungs. Then hold that breath while you count to six. Don't just let it out all at once, but exhale slowly, counting once more to six. Then repeat, and continue to do this for several minutes. You'll start to feel better in no time.

 You can boost the value of deep breathing by chanting to yourself, "In with the good" on the inhalations, and "Out with the bad" on the exhalations. It's a simple way to rid your mind of toxins.

 Talk to a friend or a loved one. Don't keep things bottled up inside of you. Sometimes all it takes is a word or two with somebody near and dear to make things feel right again. If it's not your friend or your wife or your husband or your sister or brother or aunt or uncle, then maybe it's a clergyman or your family doctor or anyone who feels right.

 Developing your spiritual side can be really helpful in dealing with stress. I didn't grow up with any

religion, but I started going to this church with a great gospel choir right here in my neighborhood, and when I sit there on a Sunday, I feel like a whole other person.

✤ There are people who specialize in helping those of us who suffer from problems with stress, and they are called "mental health personnel." There should be no stigma in seeking their counsel. For tooth problems, you'd go to a dentist; for hay fever, you'd go to an allergist. Same thing here. And it doesn't have to be a long-term commitment either. Sometimes a short intervention of five or six sessions with a mental health professional can clear up the stress that feels like such static in your life.

✤ Some people experience enormous stress relief from having a pet. Don't underestimate the value of these relationships. A walk with your dog or a cuddle with your cat can neutralize a lot of the pressures of the moment.

✤ Regular exercise is a great stress buster. Once those endorphins are released, there really isn't a better anti-stress medicine to be had.

✤ A good laugh can chase stress out of your day. Get yourself some good comedy tapes, and listen to them on the commute home. You'll feel a lot better. As a matter of fact, a friend of mine gave me some Loretta La Roche tapes for the car. She's this advocate of laughter as therapy, and she's very funny and very real. You can check out her Web site at <http://www. stressed.com>.

❦ A vacation may be just what the doctor ordered. Americans don't take nearly enough vacation time. In Europe, everybody takes at least a month off in the summer. Here we're crazy workaholics, where stress is regarded as a normal, even a positive, thing. Don't buy into that.

❦ Who says a vacation has to cost money? To me, a vacation is anything that breaks the pattern that's causing you stress. Take a few days off, stay home, build a birdhouse, go to the beach, bake a cake, catch a French movie in the afternoon—you'll see how much better you'll feel very soon.

We now move on to our next chapter, a vital subject in the lives of all who work in the hotel and motel field: safety and hygiene.

Chapter References

National Highway Traffic Safety Administration data accessed June 2004 at <http://www.my.webmd.com/content/article/64/72426.htm?printing-true>

Sleep deprivation research accessed June 2004 at <http://www.sinc.sunysb.edu/class/psych35801/slider/lecture6_0217.pdf>

Chapter 7

Safety First

Back in the old days, when the lodging industry first came into being, inns and other such hostelries were considered dangerous places where people of virtuous character who happened to find themselves on the road had to fend off potential thieves, drunkards, and other characters of ill repute. Food and bedding were unclean. Straw palettes could burst into flames. Rats and mice scurried underfoot. And there was no *Zagat* on which to rely for appraisal of these lodgings. A traveler might literally be risking his or her life upon stumbling into the wrong place.

Jump ahead to the twenty-first century. Today's travelers who journey to faraway locations can feel secure staying in "name-brand" hotels, or they can use tour books and guides to find out which independent hotels come highly recommended. Hotels that are not recommended might turn out to be pleasant surprises, or they might turn out to have cramped, dark rooms, lots of noise, and unsavory characters, just as the inns of long ago.

Some of us have been lucky enough to be guests at hotels that feel absolutely luxurious, where our every wish is met and our every need is anticipated. Sometimes we take it down a notch and stay at comfortable, safe hotels that feel a little like "a home away from home," and those are quite wonderful too. Then, of course, a great many of us stay at the "name-brand" hotels or motels—the Hilton, Marriott, Days Inn, Ramada, and so forth—where we pretty much know what to expect and, for the most part, we get it. Some of us choose to restrict ourselves to the tried-and-true places when we're traveling, whereas others among us travel with a more adventurous spirit and want to "taste" the culture of the country we are visiting, thus we seek out small hostels and *pensiones*. When traveling in our own country, we may prefer to stay at inns and B&Bs rather than at commercial hotels. Most of us, however, have had the unfortunate experience of staying at places that fell far below the mark, and these mistakes particularly stick in our minds. Let's hear from some of your colleagues about the places at which they wish they *hadn't* stayed.

I once had my pocket picked in a hotel in Chicago. It was a very well-known hotel, and they were having a convention there. No, it was not a convention of petty thieves. But the point is that the hotel didn't exercise adequate security to monitor who was going in and out during that period. So I was robbed of $200, and my peace of mind was shot to ribbons.

 I was once in Minneapolis on business, and a mouse ran across the bathroom floor. They must have heard me scream in St. Paul. I guess you can't blame a mouse for wanting to be indoors in Minneapolis in December, and I did get upgraded to a much nicer suite, but even so, I never felt secure there again and didn't sleep well for the three days I stayed.

 The worst time I've ever had in a hotel was in the Bahamas. I was staying at a resort and another single woman who was staying there was raped. I flew home the next day. I just couldn't handle the idea of being there. It later turned out that one of the staff did it. Unbelievable . . .

For every horror story mentioned above, we could easily come up with 10 more. There are a lot of bad hotels. So if these bad experiences are so universal, the question, becomes, why do they happen and, more to the point, what can the hotel and motel industry do to ensure that its establishments are safe and clean for both guests and employees?

Hygiene and Sanitation

One of the most notorious cases in the annals of the hotel and motel industry was the outbreak of Legionnaire's disease that occurred in the summer of

1976 at a hotel in Philadelphia. The Pennsylvania Division of the American Legion was holding a convention, and of the hundreds of conventioneers who attended the meeting at the convention center hotel, 221 became ill. Within two to four days of having been at the hotel, these guests developed high fevers, chills, headaches, and muscle aches. These initial symptoms gave way to a host of more serious ones, such as dry cough, chest pains, shortness of breath, mental confusion, and diarrhea. All of these cases eventually developed into pneumonia, and ultimately 34 fatalities occurred among the 221 people who fell ill. After much detective work, it was determined that all of the cases were linked to having showered in water that had been pumped out of the hotel's faulty hot water system.

In recent years, Legionnaire's disease has resurfaced in a variety of hotel settings, while similar illnesses have broken out frequently on cruise ships . . . also known as "floating hotels." The danger of developing a fatal illness from some aerosolized pathogen is slim indeed when you consider how many people visit hotels every year, but the point of the story will always be relevant. It is very important for all of those who enter the hotel and motel field to understand that while people are your guests, you are *taking care of them.* Taking care of them means that you bring them big fluffy towels and frosty cocktails and you turn their beds down—or whatever service standard your establishment sets—but you are also taking care of them in the sense that you are keeping them safe and out of danger as best you can. That is part of your unwritten oath, and it can never be forgotten nor neglected.

So what are the areas of risk? Let's take a look.

Food Service

The great majority of hotels and motels, from the biggest resort to the smallest B&B, serve food, at least to some extent. And when food is served, danger is present. According to the U.S. Public Health Service, more than 40 diseases are food transferable. In other words, we should all be very careful about what we put into our mouths. Hotel and motel professionals should be absolutely attentive to the standards that protect guests from food-related risks. The cost of error is high. Not only is there the potential for human tragedy, but there also is the issue of liability. A few sick people who can point to your hotel as the site of their infection can completely wipe out your business.

We tend to think of food-borne illnesses as being incubated in greasy spoons and other unsavory, low-end establishments, but the truth is, food-borne illnesses can happen anywhere. As far as we're concerned, we'd choose a nice clean diner any day over a four-star restaurant that takes shortcuts when it comes to hygiene and sanitation. Food-borne illnesses such as hepatitis A and salmonella can and do kill people, but the good news is that they can largely be prevented through the practice of good sanitation habits. First things first, however: when it comes to hygiene and sanitation, the place to begin is with *you.* Consider the section that follows to see whether you're being as careful as you need to be.

Food Borne Illnesses: An Overview   A quick overview of the more widespread and serious of these illnesses can be found in the chart below.

Personal Hygiene

Somewhere along the way, you may have heard of Typhoid Mary, whose given name was Mary Mallon.

Illness	Incubation Period	Symptoms	Suspect Foods
Hepatitis A	30 days, average	Diarrhea; dark urine; jaundice; flulike symptoms (i.e., fever, nausea, headache, abdominal pain)	Shellfish harvested from contaminated waters; raw produce; uncooked foods; cooked foods not reheated after contact with infected food handler
Norwalk-like viruses	24–48 hours	Nausea; vomiting; watery, large-volume diarrhea	Poorly cooked shellfish; ready-to-eat foods touched by infected workers; salads; sandwiches; ice; cookies; fruit

Continued

Illness	Incubation Period	Symptoms	Suspect Foods
E. coli	1–8 days	Severe diarrhea that is often bloody; abdominal pain and vomiting	Undercooked beef, unpasteurized milk and juice; raw fruits and vegetables; salami; salad dressing; contaminated water
Listeria	9–48 hours for gastrointestinal symptoms; 2–6 weeks for invasive disease	Fever, muscle aches; nausea and diarrhea	Fresh, soft cheese; unpasteurized milk; deli meats; hotdogs
Salmonella	1–3 days	Diarrhea; fever; abdominal cramps; vomiting	Contaminated eggs, poultry, unpasteurized milk or juice, cheese, and contaminated fruits and vegetables
Shigella	24–48 hours	Abdominal cramps; fever; diarrhea	Food or water contaminated with fecal matter

She was the first person found to be a "healthy carrier" of typhoid fever in the United States. This meant that Mary had no outward signs of illness but could infect others, which she did . . . in spades. In 1906, Mary started working as a cook for a wealthy New York City family that was spending the summer on Long Island. Every member of the family came down with typhoid fever, and eventually, the outbreak and the subsequent deaths of 47 people were traced back to . . . that's right, Mary. Her name went down in infamy. Surely you don't want your name—or the name of your hotel—to go down in infamy too. So, then, what do you need to do to safeguard your good name? You need to follow, as conscientiously as possible, certain rules regarding good hygiene. Of course, these rules are absolutely non-negotiable if you are in any way involved with food, but all of us can profit from following them in general. Let's hear how your colleagues go about ensuring good hygiene.

👑 I'm the director of rooms for a hotel in Corpus Christi, Texas, and we've instituted a policy that every one of our employees undergoes regular physical examinations. I think it's important to act preventively rather than reactively. Picking up a case of hepatitis before it enters the general population is just good practice. Keep in mind too that our industry is reliant on making hires from other countries, especially developing countries where there may be a high incidence of tuberculosis or AIDS or whatever. Regular examinations— particularly incoming examinations—also help to protect your establishment against any disability claims where the employee says the disability was incurred on the job, and you know very well it wasn't.

❦ I'm the director of services for a resort in Maui. I regard it as part of my job to look at people critically. (This is different from criticizing people.) But we have certain standards to maintain, and when one of my staff shows signs that those standards are not being met—whether it be a soiled uniform, a noticeable body odor, dirty hands, noticeable scratching, frequent sneezing—I have to deal with this in some way. At the very least, I have to remind the person that we do have standards for appearance. Beyond that, I have to make sure that the person is not carrying around something infectious that could be a risk to other staff members or to guests.

❦ If you wear a uniform, make sure it's a clean one. There is an aesthetic consideration involved—obviously clean uniforms look and smell a lot nicer than dirty ones—but there's also an issue of germs. Careful laundering of your uniform in hot water will help keep harmful microbes at bay.

❦ As a general manager, I make it a point to model good grooming. That means that my nails are always trimmed, my hair is neat, I'm not awash in aftershave or cologne, my clothes are clean and pressed, and my shoes are shined. At those times in my life when I've had a beard, I've been scrupulous about keeping it trimmed and neat. Neatness counts—don't ever let anyone tell you differently.

❦ I believe that anyone who deals in service has to understand how important it is to keep the hands washed. Not just for the protection of guests, but to protect yourself as well. Working in a hotel, you're going to come into contact with many people in the course of the day, and let's not forget that in this day and age, somebody can get on a plane in Egypt or Malaysia or wherever, carrying some exotic microbe, and 12 hours later they're standing in the lobby of your hotel touching your hand as you give out the room key. If you wash your hands frequently, everyone will be a lot better off.

Wash Those Hands

Medical science made a great breakthrough hundreds of years ago when physicians recognized the connection between the conscientious washing of hands by medical personnel and the reduced mortality rates among patients. The same precautions apply to anyone who serves the public, so that means you'll need to learn the proper techniques for hand washing.

When to Do It:
Always take a few moments to wash your hands

- before starting work.
- after using the lavatory.
- after handling raw food.
- after touching your hair, coughing, sneezing, blowing your nose, or touching any type of waste or refuse.
- often during the day, as it occurs to you. You cannot *overwash* your hands!

How to Do It:

Follow these steps, and you'll be doing it right:

- Rinse your hands.
- Wash hands thoroughly with an approved soap.
- Rub the soap through your fingers and thumbs and all over your palms.
- Rinse thoroughly.
- Use a paper towel or a hot air dryer to dry your hands.
- Turn off the tap with a paper towel.

One other thought. Do you remember those times when you've been to the dentist and the hygienist gave you this special rinse to swish around in your mouth? All of the parts you missed came out blue, didn't they? Well, a similar product exists that can be useful in training staff regarding hygiene and sanitation issues. It's a special powder that you put on your hands. After you've washed, you look at your hands in infrared light. Any place the powder glows blue is one that was missed during hand washing. A picture tells a thousand words!

Safe Food Handling

For those in the hotel and motel field who are primarily involved in food service, we offer a companion volume to this book, *A Survival Guide for Restaurant Professionals.*

In it we discuss in greater depth some of the food-handling issues we are exploring here. Many of you who are entering this field, however, may find yourself involved in some aspect of food service at some point in your career. Many general managers and resident managers and even directors of marketing or human resources started in the hotel business working as a beverage manager or as a waiter or chef. In fact, it is a wonderful thing for a general manager to learn all aspects of the hotel business firsthand, so a tour of duty on the food service end of things makes great sense. Again, however, if you're going to be in food service, even for a little while, you have to know the rules. Here are some of them, right from the horse's mouth:

👑 Before I say anything else, I just want to stress the importance of *looking* at the environment you're in. And I'm talking about doing this both as a patron, if you stay at a hotel, or as an employee, if you're working there. Does it feel okay to you? Does it smell okay? Are there smudges on the glasses or lipstick stains on the cups? Does the food on the buffet table look wilted and tired? Does the staff take shortcuts? If you're not finding satisfactory answers to these questions, then you have no business being in such a place . . . either as a guest or as a member of the staff. Go find some other place that's better for your health.

👑 Any hotel or lodging that offers dining, whether it is in a restaurant setting, a café, or a banquet facility, must understand the importance of proper food storage. Most of us now understand that certain foods simply do not keep well. We've all heard about the perils of poultry stuffing, for instance, or egg salads and potato salads that are kept unrefrigerated. Some fancy buffets feature dishes that are made with aspic, which can be very beautiful to look at, but an important ingredient in aspic is agar-agar, the very material that's used in the lab to grow cultures, so just imagine how well bacteria does growing in this fancy preparation.

As director of engineering, I have responsibility for my hotel's entire physical plant. The issue of food safety is always at the front of my brain. I check the counters in the kitchen, for instance. Are there any nicks in the surfaces, or any parts of the counter that could be penetrated by substances that might harbor bacteria? (Kitchen counters should be constructed of marble or stainless steel so that they cannot be easily penetrated.) What kind of condition are the garbage cans in? Are they kept clean? Inside and out? The point I'm making is that you have to have a roving eye and find the problem before it finds you.

As food and beverage director of a hotel in Winnipeg, I've set down the rule that rare meats are a thing of the past. One outbreak of E. coli could end our business, so it's bye-bye to black-and-blue steak. If you have any kind of involvement with food at all, keep yourself informed about any new guidelines with regard to the suggested internal temperatures for meat, fish, poultry, and so forth.

Is your refrigeration cold enough? I remember hearing about a restaurant where an outbreak of staph occurred because the coconut custard pies were stored

in the refrigerator only at a temperature between 52°
and 60°.

✿✿✿ When I came on as the catering manager for the
hotel I'm in now, we were doing a buffet lunch and I
saw one of the staff refilling a serving dish that had
held a crabmeat salad. I almost jumped out of my skin.
Right after that lunch, I gathered everyone together
and drilled it into them that when a serving dish is
empty on a buffet table, you must always clean it out
before adding more food. Better yet, start with a fresh
dish altogether.

The "Top 10" Rules for Bacteria Control

Bacteria are living organisms. That means they
require food, moisture, the proper pH, and time to
grow. They particularly love foods that are high in
protein, such as dairy and meat, and they *really* love
eggs, fish, and shellfish. They also can't resist may-
onnaise, hollandaise sauce, custards, and other egg-
filled treats.

Our "Top 10" tips for control follow:

1. Heat foods to an internal temperature of
   140°.

2. When holding food, make sure you maintain the 140° internal temperature.

3. Only heat small quantities at a time. When
   you heat large quantities, it is difficult to maintain consistency of temperature throughout.

---

4. Heat foods rapidly.

5. Heat foods close to the time you'll be serving them.

6. Never use a steam table to reheat foods. Heat them rapidly to the internal temperature recommended, and then transfer them to the steam table.

7. To chill hot foods quickly, put them in an ice bath or under cold, running water.

8. When placing cooked foods in the refrigerator, always place them above uncooked food. This will prevent cross-contamination.

9. *Never* thaw foods at room temperature. Thaw them in the refrigerator in a container so they don't drip their contents onto other foods.

10. Use your head!

If you really want to get a sense of what can go wrong, observe people dining at a buffet some day. You'll probably see people putting their hands into serving bowls to pick out an olive or a grape. The possibilities for cross-contamination are everywhere. Instruct your staff that all serving spoons and tongs and ladles have to be cleaned and sanitized every half hour. Or, to play it even safer, replace them with fresh ones.

Never use cans that are rusted, corroded, or that bulge suspiciously. They could be harboring botulism, which will spell the end of your business . . . if not the end of a few lives as well. Also, make sure that cans are rinsed or wiped off before you open them. There could be mouse droppings or corrosion that would damage the contents.

The "V" Word

That's "V" for "vermin" . . . and nothing will ruin the reputation of your establishment faster than the sudden appearance of unwanted mice, rats, and cockroaches. Each person who works in a hotel or motel, from house-keeping to payroll, should have her or his antennae up—excuse the expression—for telltale signs that unwanted visitors are present. These telltale signs include:

Droppings. Not to be confused with cumin seeds, these small, dry, black spherical items are, in fact, mouse droppings. Rat droppings are larger and moist when fresh.

Damage. It is a rodent's purpose in life to gnaw, and gnaw it will, through just about anything. If you come across signs of gnawing—on foods, but also on wood, soap, or even pipes—you'll know that these critters are lurking.

Smears. We know—this discussion is getting truly gross. Smears are the ugly marks left behind when the greasy, dirty fur of a rodent comes into contact with kitchen surfaces.

Disappearance of bait. Here today, gone tomorrow can only mean one thing. There's a mouse (or worse) in the house.

What do you do if you see any of the aforementioned? Try the following measures: (1) Remove any hiding places, such as cartons, crates, or other forms of rubbish; (2) Fill rodent holes with steel wool, concrete mixed with glass, or other such impenetrable materials;

Creepy Crawlies

High on the list of things you don't want anywhere near your hotel or motel are cockroaches. They're ugly, they're dirty, they're smelly, and they carry bacteria such as *Shigella* and *Salmonella*. In truth, they don't spread disease nearly as much as houseflies, but even so, they're just horrible. Call in a professional exterminating service at once to deal with these unwanted visitors.

Another pest that is staging a comeback in the United States is the bedbug. Chances are, you have never seen a bedbug, and if you know of its existence at all, you probably think of it as something that went the way of the Model T or the icebox. In fact, this little, flat, beetlelike creature that lives in mattresses and comes out to bite sleeping guests is back, due to an upswing in international visitors from countries where the bedbug is still prevalent. These visitors can bring bedbugs into your hotel or motel via their luggage. No, you can't conduct luggage searches, but you can call in an exterminator upon the first sighting of these noisome pests.

---

(3) Store all food in rodent-proof containers. And, most important, call an exterminator! If a rat runs across your lobby, you can kiss your bookings good-bye.

Accident Prevention

In order to protect against accidents, your hotel or motel needs to institute an overarching policy, and it needs to train its workers. Some useful ideas on the subject from those in the field follow.

Cuts

Accidents with knives and other sharp tools can pose a big problem.

👑 Require any member of the kitchen brigade who uses a knife to wear a special woven glove that's designed to eliminate cuts. Have enough of these gloves on hand to designate some for poultry, some for meats, and some for fruits and vegetables. Follow manufacturers' instructions on how to sanitize them.

👑 A sharp knife is safer than a dull knife, which makes you work harder and apply more pressure. The harder you're forced to work, the more likely you are to slip.

👑 All cutting should be done on a cutting board or other hard surface. Don't ever cut anything holding it in your hand.

✠ Never cut with the knife blade facing your body, and always make sure that your hands are dry when using a knife.

✠ Always carry knives point down.

✠ Don't try to catch a falling knife. You're not a circus performer.

✠ There's a right way to do something and a wrong way. Don't take shortcuts. Don't tell yourself, "Well, I've got this knife in my hand anyway—why bother with a church key when I can just pry the lid off that jar with this?" What's wrong with that picture? Well, maybe you'll have time to figure it out on the way to the emergency room.

✠ Here's an accident that's waiting to happen: trying to slice frozen food. That's just plain crazy. Wait for the food to thaw, and *then* slice it.

Burns

Where there's smoke, there's fire. Where there's fire, there's the potential for burns.

✠ Rule #1: Make sure your fire extinguishers work!

✠ Always keep oven mitts handy. The best oven mitts I've found are welding gloves that you can buy at the hardware store or an auto supply shop. They're made of thick, heat-resistant leather and come with long, gauntletlike cuffs that protect your wrists. Because they're designed to be worn while you work with your hands, they offer lots of control and flexibility. And they're cheap.

🐝 Grease fires can be pretty terrifying. Never fill a deep fryer to more than a third of its capacity. Also, any deep fryer you use should have a lid in case things veer out of control.

🐝 When you take the lid off a pot, always lift up the far edge of the lid first. You could scald yourself if you do it the other way around.

🐝 When adding food to hot oil, make sure that the ingredients are dry. Blot any moist ingredients, because the water will make the oil spatter, and you could be burned.

🐝 Stand well to the side when you're opening an oven door, as 500° hitting you square in the face can really hurt.

🐝 If you want to check an item that's in the oven, pull out the rack first. Don't reach in to get the item. The interior of ovens are very hot, remember?

🐝 In the event of a fire on a range, turn off the heat immediately. Cover the pan or douse it with salt or baking soda (baking *soda*, not baking *powder*, which could make the fire worse). Under no circumstances should you try to douse the fire with water or a Class A fire extinguisher. These will make the grease spatter, and you could be very badly burned. If the fire is in an oven, a broiler, or a microwave, turn off the appliance

It's a Gas

Proper handling of gas is another thing that must be kept in mind when you're working in a kitchen. Remember the following precautions:

👑 One of the scary things that can happen in a kitchen is a gas leak. As soon as you smell gas, turn off the stove, open the windows, and have everyone go outside. Then call the gas company . . . from outside.

👑 If you're ever relighting a pilot light, here's something very important to remember: light the match first, then turn on the gas to light it. Don't do it the other way around, because that gives the gas a chance to accumulate while you're striking the match.

at once, or disconnect it from its power source. Keep the door closed until the fire goes out. If you can't put the fire out easily, call the fire department immediately.

👑 Never try to carry a pot or pan with burning contents to the sink. You could burn yourself or drop the pan, causing an even bigger fire.

Toxicity

As a society, our use of chemicals is often excessive.

👑 Too much exposure to chemicals can be really dangerous. It can result in allergic or immunological reactions. It's easy to develop something like contact dermatitis, for instance, from chemicals. Think about experimenting with natural substances in place of some of those potentially damaging chemicals. Lemon peel or cinnamon sticks steeped in water can be a lot nicer and safer than those so-called "air fresheners." Maybe you can use baking soda to clean a surface instead of some caustic scouring powder. White vinegar works wonders on most things too.

Mold and Mildew

More and more hotels and motels are being sued by claimants who say their allergic reactions were set off by mold and mildew in their rooms. Some ways to cope with these issues follow:

🦋 Prevent mold by adding mold inhibitors to paint, venting clothes dryers to the outdoors, using air conditioners and dehumidifiers in hot, humid weather, and making sure that kitchens and bathrooms have adequate ventilation.

🦋 To clean up mold, first take a picture of the damage for insurance purposes. Always use a mask or respirator before attempting cleanup, as well as protective gloves and eyewear. Remove or clean the contaminated materials in a way that minimizes the release of spores. In other words, don't use an electric sander to sand off the mold!

✥ Never mix cleaning chemicals. You might set off a chemical reaction and produce something really dangerous, like chlorine gas buildup.

Bumps and Bruises

Watch where you're going . . . always!

✥ One of the best strategies I've discovered for preventing accidents is to make sure that all my staff wear sensible footwear. Do you know how many back injuries are related to slipping? Your housekeeping and kitchen personnel should be wearing shoes with slip-resistant, rubber, or urethane soles. Your groundsmen and engineering staff should be wearing steel-toed footwear.

✥ Your staff can open themselves up to injury if they're dressed inappropriately for work. People working around machines should not be wearing ribbons or jewelry dangling from their ears or their wrists or wherever.

✥ All high-traffic doors should have a vision panel. Double-door arrangements, like those in the kitchen, should have doors that are marked IN and OUT. Just make sure that everybody knows which is which.

✥ Open drawers in the kitchen invite serious accidents.

✥ Pot handles must be turned to the rear, thank-you very much.

👑 Store heavy items on low shelves. If you're taking a heavy pot down from a high shelf, it could slip out of your hands, fall on your head, and cause major head trauma.

👑 Wipe up spills the second they happen. Spilled oil can be cleaned by sprinkling a layer of flour over the oil. Within a few minutes, the flour should have absorbed the oil. Use a paper towel (or a brush if you suspect that broken glass might be present) to move the flour around, making sure that all the oil gets absorbed, and then sweep the whole business into a dustpan. You can finish up by spraying the area with a glass cleaner.

👑 I've witnessed so-called restaurant "professionals" reaching for something up high on a chair with telephone books piled up under their feet. Great way to get yourself killed. Use real step stools, for heaven's sake. That's what they're made for.

👑 Walk, don't run. Make that the foundation of all your safety training. Put it up on the walls, stamp it on people's pay envelopes, tattoo it on foreheads.

👑 If you've got overhangs or places where people could hit their heads, outline them with some kind of brightly colored tape or some other eye-catching device.

👑 Make sure you have a good snow and ice removal program in effect. Figure out who's doing what. And until it's done, make sure you warn your guests about any dangers. A sign that says DANGER—ICY SIDEWALK is a very cheap alternative to a lawsuit.

Test Your Equipment

Sure, you've got a lot of safety equipment on hand, but what good is it all unless you maintain it and test it regularly to see that it functions as it should?

 In our hotel, all of the safety equipment is checked at least once a day. Fire extinguishers, house phones and radios, and automated external defibrillators are all checked three times a day (no kidding!). Generators are tested once a week. You can't be too careful.

 Once a year, we have an outside company come in and conduct extensive testing on our extinguishers and generator. Our smoke detectors are cleaned once a year, and a contractor maintains the fire-alarm panel on a quarterly basis.

The Big Picture

All of the above tips are useful, but it is even more useful to pay attention to the big picture and to keep thinking, all of the time, about how accidents can be prevented.

 Pay close attention to near misses. Heinrich's Law, a basic tenet of safety engineering, states that for every 330 potential accidents, 300 occur with no injury,

29 with minor injuries, and one will result in significant injury. We all need to investigate, discuss, and evaluate those near misses to see what went wrong and how the situation can be prevented in the future.

✦ Your hotel's safety policy needs to be thought out and written out so that everyone can sign onto it. In other words, easy-to-read words should be used, and the content should be bilingual, if your situation calls for it. This document should include the names of the staff members who have been made responsible for fire safety and prevention, for personal injuries, for OSHA [Occupational Safety and Health Administration] compliance, for first aid, and for safety training. If you don't already have something like this in place, what are you waiting for?

✦ You can have the best safety policies in place, but if morale is poor in your hotel, then expect accidents to happen. It's true—accidents occur when people are feeling stressed, and people feel stressed if the environment is rife with infighting and backbiting and indifference. Such places tend to be dangerous places, not just emotionally or psychologically but physically too.

✦ As a manager, pay close attention to scheduling, and make sure that people are taking their breaks. Tired people are people who have accidents . . . or who *cause* accidents.

✦ It's all about training. Training has to be kept up all the time. You can never be blasé about it. And never scrimp on safety. Better you should forego marble in the guest room bathrooms than use inadequate lighting where your staff is working. Poor lighting, poor venti-lation, too little or too much heat—that's what leads to accidents.

Interfacing with Your Inspector

Part of being in the hotel and motel business is dealing with periodic visits from inspectors who are there to ensure that you are meeting the proper standards of hygiene and safety. These visits can be nerve-wracking, but you're better off tamping down your nervousness and doing your best to develop a productive relation-ship with the inspector, whose findings can greatly benefit your operation and even point out ways to avoid making costly mistakes. Remember, too, that you and the inspector are on the same page, or should be: you both want to keep guests safe. Some tips from your fellow hotel and motel professionals follow about how to handle inspectors' visits:

☙ Try not to take things personally. The inspector is just doing his job. Listen to him instead of jumping in to make denials. What he has to say may save you a lot of trouble in the future.

☙ Ask questions if you want—the inspector won't object. These visits should be a learning experience all around.

☙ Join the inspector on his tour. Seeing the way he works will help you understand how you need to think in between visits. Bring a note pad with you, and jot down any observations as you go along. That will show how seriously you're taking this.

🦋 Don't go overboard playing "nice-nice" with the inspector. In other words, don't run after her with

---

Emergency!

All of the aforementioned tips have to do with business-as-usual safety. But what kind of plan does a hotel or motel need in the event of a major emergency, such as a natural disaster? Some useful ideas follow:

🦋 Appoint a member of the executive committee as the crisis manager for the hotel. (The director of engineering is a logical choice.) This person should train other personnel in evacuation procedures, bomb threat procedures, and responses in the event of fires and floods.

🦋 Be sure to have on hand an ample supply of emergency materials, such as flashlights and batteries, glow sticks, first-aid supplies, portable generators and fuel, and water pumps. A supply of nonperishable canned foods and potable water also is recommended. Check your equipment routinely.

🦋 Fire drills and employee-readiness procedures should be conducted at least quarterly. All new employees should be trained in emergency readiness.

---

mini-muffins or truffles or whatever. She may think you're trying to bribe her.

🐾 Watch your mouth. No matter how intensely you might disagree with the findings, restrict your responses to a follow-up letter. You certainly don't ever want to get into a screaming match with your health inspector.

This chapter is just a beginning regarding the serious issues of safety and hygiene in your hotel or motel operation. Stay informed regarding any and all new guidelines, changes in code, and so forth. You can't afford to be "just okay" on this subject. For your own sake and for the sake of your guests, you have to be the very best you can be.

Chapter References

U.S. Public Health Service data accessed June 2004 at <http://www.niaid.nih.gov/factsheets/foodbornedis.htm>

Heinrich's Law information accessed June 2004 at <http://www.ishn.com/CDA/articleinformation/features/BNP_features_item/021623244,00.html>

Chapter 8

All about the . . . Food and Drink People

Imagine this. You've pulled into some remote accommodation after driving for hours and hours, and you're absolutely famished. You're dreaming of a great big T-bone steak or a corned beef sandwich or maybe just a Western omelet but . . . what? This place doesn't even have a restaurant?! After the initial shock wears off, you weigh your options. You can get into your car and drive another 20 miles to a diner over in the next county, or you can use the vending machine off of the laundry room. Let's see now. Peanut butter and cheese crackers, malted milk balls, and a beef jerky for dinner. Pass the antacids please.

Does the aforementioned nightmare scenario sound at all familiar? We thought it might. Yes, you've been to the "Last Resort," and so have we . . . that dreadful place where your menu choices can only be accessed by a handful of coins. In an ideal world, all lodgings would offer real meals, but many of them don't. In this chapter, however, we're going to steer away from such modest lodgings and focus our attention instead on the hotels, motels, resorts, and other facilities where food represents a significant part of the overall operation.

A first-class hotel usually will feature several restaurants, a café, a lounge, possibly a breakfast room and, of course, banquet and catering services. Such facilities clearly require a significant staff to run them. Let's begin by introducing the cast of characters. The personnel that make up the food and beverage team of a full-service hotel include:

Director of Food and Beverage
1. Executive Chef
   - Sous Chef
   - Banquet Chef
   - Restaurant Chef
2. Director of Catering
   - Caterings Manager(s)
   - Banquet Manager
   - Setup Staff
   - Audio/Visual Manager
   - Convention Service Manager(s)
3. Director of Restaurants
   - Restaurant Manager(s)
   - Lounge Manager(s)

- Purchasing Supervisor
- Beverage Manager
- Storeroom Supervisor

Now that's a pretty big team. Obviously only the largest establishments have teams of such magnitude. We do not have room in this chapter to discuss all of these team players, so for information on chefs, consult *A Survival Guide for Culinary Professionals*, one of our other volumes in this series of books, where you will find many tips for chefs, *sous*-chefs, and others involved in food service. Another book in the series, *A Survival Guide for Restaurant Professionals*, offers useful information for "front of the house" personnel, such as restaurant managers and maître d's. In this chapter, however, we pay particular attention to the duties and functions of the director of food and beverage and the director of catering. Let's begin with the director of food and beverage.

The Buck Stops Here

The person who holds the very important job of director of food and beverage reports directly to the general manager. He or she is primarily responsible for all aspects of the dining rooms, the banquet service, the coffee shop, and the lounge operation. Let's hear how these folks view their job.

✤ I see my job as having two main thrusts: one is to provide the very best service and meals to our guests, and the other is to make the most profit doing that. It's a balancing act, but that's the fun of it!

✤ In order to succeed in this job, you have to be someone who really knows how to deal with people. I'm always trying to find better ways to train the people who work for me—the waitstaff and the hosts and hostesses and the cashiers. They're out there, making impressions on guests, good or bad, and ultimately those impressions will have a lot of sway in whether someone decides to become a repeat guest or not. And if you don't get enough repeat guests . . . well, I don't have to draw you a map, do I?

✤ As a food and beverage director, you have to be ready for just about anything. You've got to be in the here and now, dealing with this day and all the duties that entails, and you have to be looking ahead to the future. Maybe you're looking one month ahead, or three months ahead, or a year ahead, but this job goes way beyond just getting through the day. You need to have that vision thing going, so that you can stay ahead of your competition. Are sour apple martinis going to be the next big thing? Are you going to be the last one on the block to offer those little molten chocolate cakes right out of the oven? Are you ever going to get that fancy wood-fired pizza thing going? That's the challenge—to stay two steps ahead of the pack.

✤ You'd better like meetings if you're going to make it in this job. I'm the food and beverage director for a ski resort in Vail, and believe me, half of my time is spent in meetings. Every day I have my "BEO" meeting, or "Banquet Event Orders." Then, on a weekly basis, I've got a food and beverage meeting where I'll review what's going on with my department heads. Then I'll have an executive meeting, where I'll sit down with the general manager and others on the executive committee, like the director of marketing and the director of rooms. On a weekly basis, too, I'll have a range of one-on-one meetings with my managers to see what they're up to in their specific bailiwicks. Then, on a monthly basis, we'll have a staff meeting where we'll review our entire operations system and all of our interfacing. I've also instituted a monthly luncheon where we'll honor employees who have chalked up significant achievements of some kind or another. My staff really appreciates that kind of recognition.

Get yourself a good pair of shoes, because you're going to be doing a lot of walking in this job. I do a daily walk-through of all my food and beverage areas. I go into the kitchens and into the storerooms and into the wine cellar, and I really look to see what's going on. Don't depend on other people to tell you what's happening, and don't wait until you hear about something, because by then the problem may already have gotten too big. Put on your walking shoes, and go out prowling.

A very, very important part of your job will be to maintain the highest standards of housekeeping and sanitation. A fly in the soup will almost guarantee that you'll never see the poor guest who placed that order in your hotel again. Remember that. You're the one who has to be in charge of things. You're the one who has to make sure that the operation is acting in compliance with all local, state, and federal laws and government regulations. Don't try to pass the buck to your general manager. Do your job with the understanding that the buck stops with you.

> **Take Note**
> Knowledge of safe food handling and food service hygiene standards discussed in the previous chapter must become second nature to the director of food and beverage (as well as to everyone working under him or her). Make sure you've absorbed the information in this book on that subject, and continuously inform yourself about new and changing standards and codes.

👑 Another important aspect of the job is to maintain the security of all the food and beverage property and inventories. Some of the worst thefts and losses are in our area. Wine, cutlery, food itself . . . boy, does it add up!

👑 I can't overemphasize the importance of staying ahead of the curve. Food and beverage is an area where things become passé very, very quickly. This year's kiwi garnish looks like last year's tired parsley before you know it. It's the job of the food and beverage director to be out there, catching trends and bringing back to your operation those things that are exciting, stimulating, that have a good profit margin, and that will bring in new business.

✦ This job is really multifaceted. You have to interface with your staff on a daily basis and conduct performance reviews at regular intervals during the year. You have to really keep an eye on the business end of things and make sure that your daily performances meet your expectations and projections. You have to be out there marketing in the community. You have to administer wages and salaries and make sure that they're fair, and you have to hear grievances. The list could go on and on . . . and does!

✦ Certainly one of the most important functions of a food and beverage director is to maintain good, productive relationships with people. That means promoting a sense of teamwork among your staff and promoting a general feeling of satisfaction and well-being on the part of your guests. I pay close attention to guests' comment cards to see where we fell off the mark and to make the necessary corrections. Was the soup cold? Was the water glass cloudy? Believe me—you hear complaints every bit as specific as those.

✦ There are the overt functions of your job, and then there are the more subtle ones, like setting a standard of professionalism for your unit. To me, that means handling myself a certain way, dressing a certain way, creating a good ethical environment through the choices I make, and more.

Interacting with Guests

Our directors of food and beverage regard their contact with guests as an important part of their job. Their tasks include the following:

👑 Making sure that guests immediately receive quality attention upon their entrance to the establishment.

👑 Remedying any problems that come up regarding guests (or consulting with the general manager to sort out any problems you cannot resolve on your own).

👑 Replacing, without charge, any food or beverage that has not met with your guest's approval.

👑 Asking guests as they depart if their experience was satisfactory and inviting them to come back again.

As the director of food and beverage, you are not "above" the crowd. Your attitude toward your guests will determine how your staff behaves in this regard.

Menu Planning

Working with your chefs, you will be in charge of a vital part of the food and beverage operation—menu planning.

As the director of food and beverage, you've got the ultimate say when it comes to menu planning. And remember—the success of a food service operation begins with menu planning. You have to offer variety and value. If you're working in an institution—retirement home, school, hospital—where people are not coming and going, the issue of variety becomes even more pressing. As the F&B director, you have to ask key questions to get the best results. Does the menu make sense nutritionally? Is there a pleasing range of textures and flavors and colors and even temperatures? Do you have the equipment and personnel you need to carry out your plan?

Always provide a showstopper—the one part of the meal that everyone will remember. Most Americans are particularly inclined to remember dessert—that whole "Death-by-Chocolate" thing.

Make sure your menu has a pleasing balance. Sweet and salty. Tender and crisp. A meal should be a kind of symphony with a lot of colors and textures.

Use as much in-season food as you can. People drool over fresh corn and tomatoes and stuff like that, and why shouldn't they? Nothing tastes as good. Besides, they're so cheap when they're in season. And, by the same token, you don't offer pumpkin pie in the summer.

Garnish, garnish, garnish. The old parsley-and-radish rose bit continues to make sense, because dressing up a dish shows that you care and makes people feel special. And a big part of satisfying an appetite is speaking to the psychological needs that people bring to food.

🍴 I like to include foods that can be made well in advance and that hold well, like soups and stews and ragouts and such. These make everyone's life easier and definitely cut down on stress in the kitchen.

Purchasing

Making sound purchases is one of the most important aspects of the food and beverage director's job.

🍴 To succeed as a director of food and beverage, you'll have to have a fine, practiced hand at purchasing. How much corned beef do you need for St. Paddy's Day? What can you make with the leftover corned beef other than hash? Sure, you're getting a great deal on those persimmons, but how many people in this part of the world have ever eaten a persimmon or even care to try one? Purchasing is an art and a science. Your task is to not get stuck and to make people happy *and* to make money. Now that's a tall order!

🍴 As director of food and beverage, you have to get good at *forecasting*. I'm not talking about the weather. I mean figuring out the number of servings of each item that you think you'll need for each menu period. So how to approach the problem? For starters, it helps to have a math head. Then you need to be a bit of a historian. What was the average number of dishes ordered for that same period in the past? Then you have to take into account other variables, like whether it's a holiday or a good or bad economy or whether people are spending or not spending money. And then, of course, the game gets harder if your food service operation is new and you don't have any history to help you out with your forecasting. Then you'll have to draw on your own personal history—how long have you been doing this, and how much experience and expertise can you summon up?

🔱 It's very important in this line of work to have good product specifications. The point of product specifications is to achieve the kind of quality control you're looking for. Specifications should be detailed, in writing, and should cover issues like the amount to be purchased in the most commonly used units; the count and size of the items or units in its basic packaging; the common, trade, or brand name; the degree of maturity or stage of ripening; and things like that.

🔱 Every item that you serve in your establishment is important, but keep in mind that one of the items that leaves the most lingering impression, good or bad, is the cup of coffee at the end of a meal. Buy the best quality you can afford. These days, everyone is sipping high-end cappuccinos and lattés, so you sure don't want to be known for dishwater java. Choose a good coffee supplier, and get them to throw a good coffee-making machine into the deal. They'll often be willing to do that in exchange for your continued business.

🔱 I've been in the food and beverage area for over 30 years, working my way up from storeroom supervisor to F&B director at a large convention center hotel in Charlotte, North Carolina. I've witnessed huge changes in the eating habits of the American public. Cheese used to be "American" glop. And what about lettuce? That used to be a wedge of iceberg with orange dressing. Now we have all these beautiful mescluns and radicchios and field greens to choose from. I think the changes in the produce area represent the most exciting developments in the world of food, so an F&B manager or director has to really know produce. You have to learn what constitutes ripeness, and you have to familiarize yourself with how items are supposed to be packed. You don't want to be shortchanged or discover that a layer of beautiful figs is acting as a smoke screen for the duds underneath. Also, you need to acquaint yourself with sizes. Some fruits are sweeter when they're small, with the bigger items used mostly for display.

How much inventory should you keep on hand? If you know the answer to that, you'll be rich. Generally, when we speak of the shelf life of a food, we're talking about how long it can be stored without a loss of quality or weight. Fresh fish has a short shelf life; Tabasco™ sauce lives forever. Virtually any product that has water in it will shrink with storage (but not Tabasco™ sauce!), so there's no point in keeping a huge food inventory. You'll just tie up your dollars that way. So, as a general rule of thumb, don't keep any more inventory on hand than what you'll need to cover you from one delivery date to the next.

🐝 Be careful not to overbuy. You may think you're getting a great price on something, but that doesn't mean you should buy 100 pounds of the stuff instead of 10. Tastes change, sometimes seemingly overnight. For a while, quite a few years back, fondue was in. Then it was so out. Just because you can get a good buy on raclette cheese, it doesn't mean you want to be stuck with it, does it? Now some things never go out of style, so you won't have to worry about buying in bulk and taking advantage of good prices. Oils, syrups, liquor . . . liquor's never going to go out of style!

Working with Suppliers

A significant part of your work as a food and beverage director will be dealing with the people who supply you with your menu items—the vendors, purveyors, or, if you're going right to the source, the growers and cultivators. Some tips from your colleagues on how to form productive relationships with them follow:

🐝 How do you figure out which vendors to use? That's a good question. The answer is by their reputation, word of mouth, referrals—that sort of thing. Who's got the most reliable buzz? Who's famous for quality? Who's got the best price? Ask around before you commit to anyone.

🐝 Keep a roster of backup suppliers. You don't ever want to get stuck empty-handed. If your supplier can't get you crab in season, and that means you'll be disappointing your guests, then you need to find another supplier you can go to for backup. That's just the way it is.

👑 Working with a full-line distributor can make a lot of sense. Most of them offer very attractive specials, and they'll often provide training on how to prepare a new item. (I remember getting a lesson in cherimoyas from one of them.) You'll save time in placing and receiving your order, because with this kind of operation, everything is computerized, and the billing procedures are usually very clear and easy. I once bought chanterelles from a local grower, and as far as fungi go, they were great, but everything about the bill that these amateurs drew up was wrong.

👑 You have to be careful with some of these small growers and cultivators. You may tend to think, "Oh, well, they live up in the mountains, and it's all so clean and fresh and natural." Then there's an E. coli outbreak from their alfalfa sprouts, and the roof caves in. Be very careful at all times about whom you're ordering from!

👑 Always call around for competitive prices before you order anything. That's Rule #1.

Receiving and Storing

Receiving and storing food is a big issue in the life of a food and beverage director. Your colleagues approach this subject in the following ways:

🦀 This may sound simplistic, but when you come down to it, let's admit it: we're not talking about rocket science here. When you receive your order, you've got to *look carefully* at what you get. Count quantities. Check for any damaged containers. Keep an eye out for any items that might have to be repacked, but don't just use your eyes. Use your nose too. Your nose is your best friend when you're receiving foods, because noses are made to detect spoilage.

🦀 I always take random sample temperatures of any refrigerated or frozen foods I receive. You've got to be so careful about that. Your refrigerated foods are meant to be delivered below 40°F, and your frozen foods should come in at 0°F or below. If your thermometer tells you differently, don't accept! (And another thing: have a bunch of thermometers handy, and make sure to resanitize them between checks.)

🦀 There's no mistaking frozen food that isn't frozen right. You'll find rocky crystals of ice where there shouldn't be any, or whole solid areas of ice, like little glaciers, or discolorations on the food, or packages that have been bent out of shape by the thawing and refreezing. Just say no to these.

🦀 Check out your supplier's trucks. This is well within your rights as a purchaser. Walk into them, look around, and cast a critical eye. Are the raw meats separated from the produce and the ready-to-eat food? Are the refrigerated sections as cold as they should be? Remember—you're potentially dealing with people's *lives*, so don't be shy to ask your questions.

✠ Be careful about moisture and insect infestation in your dry goods order. Cereals, grains, dried fruits, sugar, flour, rice—all that stuff should come in dry, unbroken packaging.

✠ Date all your items. That will allow for FIFO inventory control—First In, First Out. And when you shelve the items, put the new supplies behind the older ones, so that the older ones get used first.

Unacceptable Foods

What happens if you get a bad batch of something? Here's the drill:

✠ Keep the bad stuff away from the good stuff. Your goal is to avoid cross-contamination.

✠ Pull out your purchase agreement and your product specifications so that you can back up your complaint.

✠ Never destroy evidence! In other words, do not throw away bad items or allow the delivery person to remove them until a signed adjustment or credit slip is transacted.

✠ Make a notation of the incident in your receiving log. Note the item involved, the specification that was not met, and what type of adjustment was made. If you start to see a pattern of unsatisfactory deliveries emerging, then it's time to change your supplier.

Banquets and Catering

Banquet sales, also known as "catering sales," are an important part of a hotel's food and beverage operation. For one thing, banquets can be priced higher than restaurant meals. Banquets generally come in a total package price for a group, and there is much less resistance to a high-priced banquet meal than a high-priced restaurant meal. Banquets also are planned around a guaranteed number of guests, so the issue of forecasting is much easier, and the prospect of waste is much reduced. What's more, labor costs are lower, as workers are hired for a limited period of time. On the down side of banqueting, the turnover rate in a banquet is very low, about once in four hours, compared to the turnover rate in a restaurant, where the guests in the restaurant seats might change four to eight times in an hour.

The person overseeing this area is the director of catering, who supervises a staff that will include such individuals as the catering managers, the banquet manager, the setup staff, the audio/visual manager, and the convention service managers. As the director of catering, you'll be supervising operations—everything from booking, selecting, and costing menu items to pricing, arranging for temporary help, and renting equipment. You'll supervise the preparation and service of food and refreshments, as well as the cleanup. You'll need strong organizational and time management skills in this position as well as the ability to multitask. Some tips follow from the professionals:

♛ You need to be a take-charge person. You've got to be a general, a producer, the one who solves the problems. You're going to be in charge of coordinating very big events—sometimes truly incredible galas—and that means everything has to be just right. The food and the service, of course, but we're also talking about the flowers and the lights and the gifts and the parking and the ice swan.

♛ Develop your math skills. You don't have to be an Einstein, but you can't be math phobic either. After all, you have to compute quantities and prices and ratios to do the job right.

♛ I can never understand how people wind up in exactly the wrong jobs for them. Like, if you hate children, don't be a babysitter, okay? By the same token, if you're not a people person, then being a director of catering may not be the correct fit for you either. After all, you're going to have to deal with an entire staff, plus you're going to want to be out there in the room, with a lot of face-to-face. And you may be presiding over something joyous and monumental in a person's life, like a wedding or a bar mitzvah or a testimonial dinner. If you can't rise to the emotional level of other people's celebrations, then you'd be better off in a backroom position.

♛ Be prepared to be on your feet and to run around for hours at a time, because that's what catering demands. You need a cool head, energy, and a sturdy pair of shoes.

❧ Some people thrive on problems; other people fly headlong into a panic when a problem presents itself. If you're one of the latter, you have no business working in this area, because catering and banquets are all about problems. The wrong flowers get delivered; there's an ice storm, and you have to deal with 200 cars; the air-conditioning fails; the Cornish hens are off. Whatever! The point is that you have to get through it somehow. And that doesn't mean screaming and yelling and throwing tantrums, although you will, no doubt, do your share of screaming. I like to think of it as constructive screaming—really speaking your mind so that the other party can hear you. Before I was in catering, I was an actress and, let me tell you, it's a lot like theater. A lot of screaming, a lot of running around, and a lot of joy when it comes off right. *And* the show must go on!

❧ Pricing is the name of the game. How do you approach it? Well, you've got your raw materials, your labor, your client's budget, the complexity and difficulty of the job, whether there's any rush element involved, and so on. As a rule of thumb, however, you start constructing your estimate by factoring in your ingredients, your time, and your overhead.

❧ You can be a master of pricing formulas, but that's all going to be academic unless you're also out there checking out the competition. Remember—you don't work in a vacuum. You work in a free market, and if you're charging $27.95 a head for a banquet dinner and your competitor across the street is charging $22.95 for pretty much the same menu, it's unlikely that you're going to get the job. So be out there, looking and listening and seeing what your competition is up to. To do anything less is to do half a job.

👑 When it comes to figuring in your labor costs, you have to really examine your menu. If you've got some labor-intensive preparations going on—bouillabaisse, or whatever—you have to divide your factored cost by the number of labor hours necessary to turn out the dish. With an easier menu, you can hike the price a little and make a better profit.

👑 Don't forget about a very important ingredient in your success: the people who work for you. For starters, I keep my prep staff happy by rotating tasks in the kitchen. Nobody wants to be peeling potatoes for six hours straight. I also make sure that people get and take their breaks. Fatigue reduces productivity and leads to accidents. I also see myself and others who have been with me awhile as teachers. We mentor less experienced staff and bring them along.

The food and beverage area is a wonderful and an exciting part of the hotel and motel industry, but obviously it's not for everyone. It's for people who love food and can create a feeling of excitement around it. In the next chapter we explore the guest contact staff—another group of hotel and motel professionals whose performance can have a significant effect on the quality of a guest's experience.

Chapter 9

All about the . . . Guest Contact Staff

When most "civilians" reflect on their hotel experiences, the images they conjure up very often have to do with how they were treated when they came through the revolving door . . . or even before they got to the revolving door. The people who meet and greet visitors, check them in and handle their baggage, and answer their questions about the neighborhood and where to get a good burger—these are the hotel and motel professionals known as the "guest contact staff." In this chapter, we explore the roles they play, and we offer tips on how these professionals can best succeed in their jobs.

"People" People

We recall somebody saying in the last chapter that if you don't like kids, don't be a babysitter. In the same vein, if you don't like people, don't talk your way into a job with the hotel's guest contact staff. It just won't work.

Let's begin this chapter with a look at who makes up the guest contact staff and what these specific jobs entail:

- *Resident Manager/Director of Rooms*
  This individual is at the top of this particular heap and is in charge of all functions that are related to rooms.
- *Front Office Manager*
  As the title suggests, this individual is responsible for much of the hotel's day-to-day operations, including the activities of the front desk, the bell-staff, and the concierge staff.
- *Front Desk Supervisor and Front Desk Staff*
  These people are support personnel for the front office manager.
- *Bell Captain*
  This is the leader of the bellstaff.
- *Valet/Garage Supervisor*
- *Valet/Garage Staff*
- *Concierge*
  This individual helps guests with a variety of things, such as securing tickets for theater or

sporting events; finding babysitters; making reservations for airlines, other hotels, car rentals, and restaurants; and giving driving directions and other information about the surrounding area.

The space limitations of this chapter prevent us from discussing the work of all the aforementioned personnel, so we will focus on the front desk staff, the concierge, and, to a lesser degree, the bellstaff. Let's start with the latter, as they are the ones who greet the guests.

The Bellstaff

If a hotel has valet or garage parking, the very first impression a guest will receive will be of whoever is parking the car. Not all hotels have valets, and not all hotels have doorpersons either, who would be the next logical people to greet guests. Now that we think about it, not all hotels today even have a bellstaff, but all first-class hotels still do. Let's hear what the members of the bellstaff have to say.

🔔 I've come up in the ranks. After I left Panama, I worked for years as a bellhop in and around Miami. Now that I've become a bell captain, I'm happy to say that I love my job. It pays well, and there's a lot of responsibility. The biggest part of my job is training and supervising the bellhops. A lot of them are very green kids, like I was, often from another country. I've got staff from Laos, Honduras, Indonesia, Somalia—

you name it. Very diverse, but they've all got one thing in common: personality. To tell you the truth, I don't care how much a person knows. Anyone can learn this job. But you've got to have personality, you know what I mean? You're dealing with people. You've got to know how to smile and make a person feel welcome, and that's a personality thing. If someone comes to me looking for a job, and they don't know how to look a person in the eye, I'm not going to say, "Hey, isn't this kid going to make a great bellhop?"

👑 If I had to pick out one aspect of my work as a bell captain that I enjoy the most, I think I would have to say it's the scheduling. Every day, I review the arrivals and departures reports—how many guests are due to arrive; how many are due to depart—and the future occupancy forecasts and, based on those, I schedule my staffing. I go by the general rule that I need one bellperson for every 75 arriving or departing guests (at more luxurious hotels, the rule of thumb might be one bellperson to 40 or 50 guests). It's a kind of fun challenge to get the numbers right.

👑 As a bell captain, you're obviously dealing with a staff that is heavily invested in receiving their gratuities. That means you have to make sure that all members of your staff get an equal number of "fronts"— a front being the escorting of a guest to his room— because that's where the tips are. The "lasts"—things like delivering messages or flowers—don't always result in a tip, so you have to keep track of who's doing what so that it all comes out fair.

✠ I'm a bellhop in one of the biggest hotels in Toronto, and I really enjoy my job. I think it's totally cool to be meeting people from all over the world. I just want to say, though, that it helps in this kind of job to be a "people person." You should be friendly and outgoing. You greet the guests, you show them to their rooms, you explain how to operate the night-lock or the television or whatever, and you really engage with them. And I don't just mean for the sake of the gratuity, although that's nice. I mean, you do it because that's the job. The job is to make the guest feel welcome and good, no matter what.

✠ Your job is to serve. You're in a service profession. Don't ever forget that. If you have a problem with that, then it's your problem. There's no indignity in serving other people. I pick up guests' clothing to be laundered or repaired; I page guests in the lobby; I deliver messages; and sometimes I deliver room service orders. And I feel like I get decently compensated for it. I am very happy with what I do, and so are my superiors. It all works out well for everyone.

✠ Keep your smile up, and work on your friendly greetings. That's how you tell your guests that they're welcome in your hotel, and that you're glad to be of service.

✠ I've met some fantastic people working in this job. We had a rock star staying with us—I won't say who—but I helped him find a ring he was missing (it was under the sofa), and he gave me this amazing leather jacket right out of his own luggage as a gift. Now that was something!

Save Your Back

According to the U.S. Bureau of Labor Statistics, more than 1 million workers in the United States suffer back injuries every year. Proper lifting techniques and other precautions will protect baggage handlers who are lifting heavy items. Keep the following in mind:

🔱 When you're going to lift a heavy load, stand close to the load with your feet spread apart about shoulder width. Keep one foot slightly in front of the other for balance. Then squat down, bending at the knees. *Do not bend at the waist.* Tuck your chin in while keeping your back as straight as possible. Get a firm grasp on the load before you lift it. Slowly begin to lift, using your legs by straightening them. Do not twist your body during this step—that's important. Once you've lifted the load, keep it as close to your body as possible. This reduces lumbar stress.

🔱 Wearing a back support belt might be helpful, but don't rely on it more than you should. It's not magic. You still have to follow proper lifting techniques.

🔱 As a bell captain, I've introduced physical conditioning and stretching programs into our staff training. This is a good way to prevent back injuries and muscle strain. I also caution my bellhops against smoking. When you smoke, the nicotine constricts the flow of blood to the discs which cushion your vertebrae. This can lead to stress and injury.

❦ Don't forget, you have to look nice. You may not be at the top of the heap, but you are still reflecting the image of the hotel, and that means your hair should be groomed, your nails should be clean, you have to smell nice, and your uniform must be clean and pressed. Don't wait for your boss to tell you to straighten up your act. Be aware of it yourself.

❦ You need to learn to listen and to communicate so that other people will want to listen to you. Communication plays a big role in this job. You need to follow the instructions that your captain gives you—that's all about communication. You need to be able to answer the questions that your guests ask you—that's communication. Without the communication skills, you'll only be doing half the job, and that just isn't enough.

❦ Important: You'll be lifting luggage and bags, so make sure you do it the right way. You don't want to hurt your back.

 *The Front Office*

The front office, also known as the "front desk," is widely regarded as the nerve center of the hotel. The front office supervises the availability of rooms, does the bookings, registers the guests, checks out the guests, and handles the keys and the mail. Front office personnel inform guests about activities in the hotel and answer their questions on everything from currency to sightseeing to where to get a good haircut. The size of the front office obviously corresponds to the size of the operation. A small off-the-road motel often may have a front office staff of one, while big-city hotels and resorts can have a sizable cadre of front office workers. No matter how big or small the front office staff may be, however, the principles of service that make this part of the hotel and motel operation effective remain consistent. Let's start with the functions of the front office.

Check-in

Checking in guests and getting them into their rooms quickly is the #1 priority of the front office. Our professionals in this area have some strong ideas about how the process should work.

👑 I've gone from being a front desk clerk to a rooms controller. That means I'm in charge of blocking. If you don't know what that is, you should, because it's an important part of front office work. It means matching up rooms with guests on the basis of the guest's preferences. The classic example of this is smoking/non-smoking. If you inadvertently book a non-smoking guest into a smoking room, then you've ruined that person's stay. It's as simple as that. So what I do is I match up the arrivals reports with the rooms inventory. I make sure that we have enough stuff on hand like rollaway beds and cribs and so forth. I handle VIP needs. I do everything I can to make sure—in advance—that the stay is going to work out to the guest's liking.

✿ As the director of rooms for a first-class hotel in Las Vegas, I manage everything having to do with rooms and, believe me, it's a big job. Sometimes you might hear me being referred to as the "resident manager." This term comes from the fact that, in the past, the resident manager actually used to live in the hotel . . . in other words, he or she was *in residence.* You had to be available at all hours to deal with everything and anything that came up, so living in the hotel made sense. Nowadays, that live-in requirement is no longer factored into the job, but it's still a highly demanding position where you can be called upon at all times of the day and night. Anyway, one of the first things I did when I took on this job was to set down the 10 x 10 rule for all of my staff. What does that mean? It means that a guest's experience staying in your hotel will largely be determined by how he or she is treated in the first 10 minutes of the stay. Since the first 10 minutes is usually spent at the front desk, you can see how important the front desk is. The other "10" in the 10 x 10 rule comes from the idea that you greet the guest 10 feet before he or she reaches you. Going *to* the guest rather than having the guest come to you makes all the difference.

✿ I've been on the front desk for about 15 years now—I work in a resort in Tucson—and I know the drill backwards and forwards. First thing I do is I verify the guest's name and the spelling of the name. Once

I pull up the reservation, I read it to the guest and confirm the specifics. "You requested a rollaway bed, Mr. Johnson?" "You're leaving on Tuesday?" "The rate is $120 per night." Then I determine if the guest is a member of our guest loyalty program, or if he's got any promotional tie-ins or coupons or whatever. Once the method of payment is determined, I issue the room key. By the way—*never speak the room number out loud.* If the guest requires assistance, I'll then summon the bellstaff.

👑 When you're registering guests, you're doing more than just putting information into a computer or handing out a key. You're trying to ensure that your guest is going to have a good stay. That means, for instance, if your guests are an elderly couple who have been booked into a room next to a group of frat boys, then you should peruse your room inventory and see what you can do to make a switch before the complaints start. The other thing is that when you're working the front desk, you're also acting as a sort of salesperson. What I mean by that is that if you spot an opportunity to upgrade someone to a better room, then do it. Let's say you've got honey-mooners checking in and you see that you have a room with a gorgeous view on a top floor that's just become available. What do you do? You bring it to the attention of the lovebirds, of course. Chances are, for this once-in-a-lifetime event, they'll be happy to upgrade from a third-floor room to a 30th-floor room. In fact, they'll probably feel like you've done them a huge favor.

Houston, We've Got a Problem . . .

Like everywhere else in the world, problems will come up, on a regular basis, around front office activities. Routine problems—such as reservation cards disappearing, rooms going unblocked, even though the guest may insist that he made a reservation—and those problems that can't be anticipated. Don't panic. Instead, offer solutions.

👑 It's so nice for everybody involved when you've got space available and you can reassign a guest to another room without his ever knowing there was a problem. But life isn't always that kind. If you're fully booked, then you've got to start digging to discover the root of the problem, maybe with the help of the reservationist. Was there a date or name mix-up? If the two members of the couple have different surnames, maybe they forgot whose name they reserved in. Stay at it until you solve the mystery, and just keep telling yourself that there's always an answer.

👑 If you're lucky, maybe you'll come up with a "sleeper"—an available room that doesn't show up on the computer. If all else fails, and there are no good rooms to be had, offer a not-so-good room— like something adjacent to a renovation, let's say, that you weren't planning to book. Offering it at a nice discount smoothes the edges on the situation and, besides, it's better than nothing.

👑 When all else fails, you've got to "walk the guests." That means calling up your contacts at other hotels in the area and getting the poor people a room. Even if it's clear that the confusion stems from the guest, you still need to do what you can to help. Not only is it good form but in the future the grateful guests may repay your kindness with a visit to your hotel.

👑 While you're working through the problem, give your harried guests a nice place to sit and offer refreshments. After all, they're bound to be upset. It's your job to make them feel better. A cold drink helps.

👑 Figure out what went wrong—after you've figured out how to correct it—and review the problem with your front office manager. You don't want the problem to repeat itself.

Reservations

Another vital function of a hotel's basic operations is its reservations system. Depending on their size, hotels may have a reservations manager and one or more reservations agents. The only people who should be filling these positions are those who have a clear idea of what they're doing. So many hotels today use reservationists who are not even located at the hotel site—in fact, your reservationist could be in Butte, Montana, while your hotel is in Toledo—that this job seems a bit off the subject of our book, but we will address it briefly.

🔖 For starters, you have to understand the difference between a regular reservation and a guaranteed reservation. A regular reservation is not paid for in advance, and it's not held beyond a certain specified time. A guaranteed reservation means that the guest has paid for the room—at least the first night—prior to arrival. These days, of course, most reservations are guaranteed, at least by credit card, although the card can be credited if a person cancels by a certain agreed-upon time.

🔖 It's very important to record the name of whoever made the reservation. Also, we try to confirm all of our reservations in writing, by e-mail or fax, if time permits. E-mail has really been a boon to the reservationist. I don't remember how I did my job before e-mail came along.

🔖 As a reservationist, I've found my multilingual abilities to be very useful in getting jobs. I'm Israeli, but I speak English, Spanish, Arabic, French, and Russian. I work for one of the biggest hotels in New York City, and the fact that I can communicate easily with so many different populations makes me very much in demand.

🔖 If you're going to be a reservationist, you can't be phobic around technology. It's always changing, it's always getting more sophisticated, and it's at the very heart of the reservations business. So just dive in, and keep your head above the water!

Know the Language

Like all worlds unto themselves, the front office has its own vocabulary. Familiarize yourself with the following terms and abbreviations:

EAP	Each additional person
DNA	Did not arrive (the guest, that is)
OOO	Out of order, signifying a room unsuitable for occupancy, either for cosmetic or mechanical problems
RNA	Registered but not assigned. This refers to a guest who has registered but who has not yet been assigned a room, perhaps because it is being cleaned.
OC	On change. A room that has been vacated and is scheduled to be cleaned
Slept-outs	Guests who have paid for a room but who have not slept there
DD	A double room with two double beds
Stay-overs (or overstays)	Guests who stay longer than planned

Calling the Concierge

Another very important member of the front office team is the concierge. Most finer hotels employ someone in this position, and those guests who know enough to utilize the services of the concierge will generally enjoy a much more satisfying stay.

So what exactly is a concierge? They are the men and women who can be thought of as "fixers." They know how to get almost anything done. Need a pearl button to match the one that fell off that blouse? The concierge can direct you to one. Have to take a client to this evening's sold-out performance of *Madama Butterfly*? The concierge may be able to find you a ticket.

Through the centuries, concierges have been fixtures in European hotels. It is only since the 1970s, however, that they have begun to appear in American hostelries. But they have caught on fast, and they represent a lively, interesting occupation that is attracting many men and women. Let's hear what our concierges have to say about their work.

🐚 Not only do we help the guests with their problems and their needs, but we function as significant members of the marketing team as well—at least we do in our hotel. I'm the concierge in a very exclusive small hotel in San Francisco, and I'm really the one on the team who best knows the habits of our repeat guests and VIPs. In fact, I stay in touch with many of these guests by e-mail, anticipating their visits and finding out in advance what will make these visits better. My contact with these guests represents a particularly important aspect of our overall marketing plan.

As the concierge of a hotel in Dallas, I'm pretty much a constant presence in the lobby. I have to say that although few people would realize that I serve in this capacity, I genuinely do contribute to the safety and security of our hotel. I'm constantly on the lookout for dangerous or undesirable people. And, believe me, I find them. They're everywhere!

I fill in often for front desk personnel. Most concierges that I know do the same. After all, concierges are often trained to do the check-in, plus we know the neighborhood, so we can offer our guests good information and leads.

I went from being a butler to concierge work. They're very related. They both call for a quiet discretion and an absolute dedication to serving your guests. I never let a guest down—seriously. If I can't do something myself, I have an "auxiliary" staff or friends and acquaintances who can pick up where I left off. I can't tell you the problems I've had to field. You need to know where to get a Chihuahua or a buffalo burger at two in the morning? I can do it. Granted, this is not everyone's idea of what they want to do with their lives, but for me it's fun, it's lucrative, and I have no complaints.

It pays to network with others in the concierge field. Let's say I've got a guest who's traveling from my hotel in Palm Springs to Denver on business. I can call ahead to my pal, a concierge at a top Denver hotel, and we can set up stuff for the guest so that he'll be happy and comfortable when he gets there. That kind of satisfaction means that he's bound to repeat with me and repeat with my Denver pal as well. The best way I've found to network is through Les Clefs d'or USA, the professional society of concierges. You can get so much off of their Internet site. Check it out at <http://www.lcdusa.org>.

The Concierge in History

It is thought that the term *concierge* comes from the Old French *comte des cierges*, or *keeper of the candles*. From this discrete task, the keeper of the candles evolved into the individual in charge of catering to the desires and whims of visiting nobility. In time, the concierges became the "keeper of the keys" not only at the castle but also at government buildings. The golden key—*le clef d'or*—has become the professional symbol of the concierge.

Principles of Guest Services

Although we've already addressed the subject of service in an earlier chapter, we'd like to briefly revisit it here, as it is so relevant to front office performance. As we said at the top of the chapter, the front office has the capacity to make or break a guest's experience. Let's see what's involved in "making" it.

Verbal Communication

The foundation of good guest service is the ability to hear what your guest has to say and to speak in a way your guest will understand. Some tips on how to do that follow:

As director of rooms for a hotel in Milwaukee, I urge my staff to recognize the importance of using an appropriate greeting. These are not your friends that you're greeting. You don't say, "Hey, bro, how's it hangin'?" Seriously, I bristle whenever I go somewhere and the personnel greet me too informally. "Hi, Al, how are you today?" Well, pardon me, but I'm not "Al" to them, I'm "Mr. Wurlitzer" or "Sir." Or, if I were a woman, "Madam," or perhaps "Ma'am."

Once you've established a person's name, make a point of using it. It signifies that you care about the person and appreciate the business that the person is bringing to your hotel. "How are you today, Mr. Jones?" "It's so nice to see you again, Mrs. Kirby."

You can never say "thank-you" too much— remember that.

Try to develop your listening skills. You really need to hear your guests. Don't rush ahead. Don't think about what you're going to say next while the guest is talking. Don't let your attention wander. *Be* with your guest.

Whatever you do, steer clear of hotel jargon. Using expressions like "I blocked you into a room" will mean absolutely nothing to most of your guests and will only make them feel uncomfortable.

Body Language

Nonverbal communication can be every bit as powerful as spoken communication, if not more so.

🪝 Nonverbal communication is an excellent way to reinforce your verbal communication. Sympathetic, interested nods tell the person who's speaking that you are really there with them.

🪝 Is there a faster way to communicate a message than with a smile? Don't be stingy with them. Like the song says, "Smile, though your heart is aching." Don't let your bad day become your guest's bad day.

🪝 Just as your body can convey feelings of warmth and friendliness—the smile, the nod of the head—so can it convey defensiveness or aggression. Folding your arms across your chest, frowning, shaking your head . . . these are all signals that will telegraph very quickly. And half the time you may not even be aware that you're giving off these signals. So you really have to watch it . . . or you have to ask a friend or coworker to observe you to make sure that you're not putting out such signals.

🪝 The manner in which you carry yourself, your dress, your grooming—these are all ways of communicating things about yourself. If you're sloppy or careless about your appearance, that's a message too.

Conflict Resolution

No matter how dedicated you may be to providing good service, there will inevitably come those times when communication between you and your guest breaks down and conflict results. Your guest, for instance, may not be as well versed in the art of communication as you are, and she may overreact badly to something very minor. If you're having a bad day as well, this could push you over the edge, and as disciplined as you may be, you could still overreact in return. Some good ideas follow about how to avoid that trap:

👑 Always start by listening. Don't rush into the fray with words. Words are hard to take back once they're spoken. Allow your guest to fully express what's on her mind. Look her in the eye in as neutral a way as you can manage. Don't lapse into a defensive posture. Try not to interrupt as she speaks, no matter how churned up you may feel inside.

👑 I've always been inclined to rush in with excuses. That's just the way it worked in my family growing up, and I've had to learn other ways of dealing with conflict. Excuses usually don't make a dent on the other person anyway. Apologies, yes. Excuses, no.

👑 When you're in the throes of a conflict, that's a really good time to pull out your reflective listening skills. You want to reflect back to the person what she's just said—putting all the cards on the table, as it were. "I understand that your earrings are missing, Mrs. Peterson, and that you suspect there might be theft involved." Okay—so now it's out there for everyone to see. And it's also good to reflect back your guest's emotional state, in a way that doesn't sound accusatory or patronizing. "You're very upset, and I understand," or, "I can see how angry you are." Keep your voice as neutral as you possibly can.

👑 Work quickly to offer a solution to the problem. If that means getting a plumber or a locksmith on the job in 10 minutes flat, then do it. If that's impossible, then try to soothe the angry guest with a peace offering until you can resolve the problem. A sticky bun and a cappuccino can work wonders!

👑 After you've dealt with a problem, document it. Not only will you cover yourself that way, but it will create an account of the situation that can be used constructively in the future to avoid other such situations.

Embracing Multiculturalism

Working in the front office of a hotel, you will most likely be in contact with people from many different countries and cultures, particularly if your hotel is situated in a big city or near a popular tourist attraction. These cultural exchanges can either be frustrating or very stimulating and satisfying, depending on the amount of preparation that the hotel has devoted to this issue. Some ideas follow about how to make the most of multiculturalism:

🦇 One of the first things I did as director of rooms when I took my job here in Salt Lake City was to put together a "language list." I discovered that I had a Croatian gardener, a Mexican painter, a Filipino house-keeper . . . well, the list went on and on. Between all the people who work here in our hotel "family," we've been able to summon up enough communication capa-bilities to make a great many of our foreign guests feel right at home.

🦇 It makes good sense to have on hand a book of common Q's & A's in a variety of languages. *What is the exchange rate? When is checkout? Where is the restaurant?* That sort of thing.

🦇 Keep your voice level normal. Speaking in a louder voice—I've actually seen some of my staff *yelling*—doesn't help anything when you're trying to get a for-eign guest to understand you.

🦇 You have to understand that different cultures have different body languages. Most Americans are very physical. They may reach out and touch you even when they hardly know you. If you try to do that with tourists from Japan, you'll probably scare them. Similarly, here in America, we're usually taught to look someone in the eye because if we don't, we'll appear shifty and distrustful. But in other cultures, Latin America, for instance, not looking directly at someone you consider your superior may be an appropriate form of deference.

As a bell captain, I have to teach my staff that when you're dealing with international guests, you can't just go and pick up their bags. They may consider that an invasion of privacy. You have to

Keeping Up the Training

What's the real key to front office success? Effective employee training that never stops. Giving good service doesn't come naturally to most people. It's learned behavior.

We do a lot of role-playing in our front office. First we practice our greetings, our smiles, and our eye contact. Then we take turns playing guests and staff, going through a variety of scenarios, like common conflicts, dealing with health crises, special needs, foreign guests, unruly children, and so forth. It's very effective.

You don't have to bring in highly paid consultants to do your training for you. It can be a real do-it-yourself operation. There are a lot of resources on the Internet, including such sites as the Educational Institute of the American Hotel & Lodging Association (<http://www.ei-ahla.com>), Hospitality Sales & Marketing Association International (<http://www.hsmai.org>), and HSA International (<http://www.hsa.com>). Check them out.

ask first. The front office is a great place to start—or end—your career in the hotel and motel field. Another area where you can get great experience is in the financial sector of the hotel. In our next chapter, we'll be looking at the "money people."

Chapter Reference

U.S. Bureau of Labor Statistics accessed June 2004 at <http://www.bls.gov>

Chapter 10

All about the . . . Number Crunchers

People see the world in different ways. Some look at a daisy and see a triumph of form—a yellow hub surrounded by white petals. Others behold a daisy and all they want to do is pull off its petals to find out if "he or she loves me or loves me not." And then there are those who gaze upon a daisy and immediately start to *count* the petals. These same people are inclined to count the number of legs on a spider, the number of miles it takes to go to the store and back, and the number of helpings in a liter of soda. It's just the way their minds think, and thank goodness for them, because we need people like that to make the world go around. Without the number crunchers, there would be no hotel and motel industry, not to mention any other kind of business, or government, or any other institution that requires budgets, balances, audits, and the like.

Let's begin this chapter by looking at the various individuals in the hotel and motel field whose jobs are primarily concerned with numbers. These individuals include the following:

Controller. This individual is the head accountant whose job is to manage all of the hotel's or motel's financial dealings, including planning and projections. Depending on the size of the operation, the controller may have one or more assistant controllers.

Credit manager. This person is usually found in larger hotels and motels, and deals with validating and authorizing guests' credit and collecting on overdue accounts.

Paymaster. Also known as the "payroll manager," this individual heads up the hotel's or motel's payroll division. In a large organization, this position might be situated within the human resources department.

Night audit manager. This person is in charge of reconciling the hotel's or motel's daily activities and transactions.

General cashier. This person is employed within the accounting department and maintains the hotel's or motel's cash supply. The cashier audits all individual bank accounts to make sure that proper accounting procedures have been followed.

Revenue manager, or **yield manager.** This is the person who specializes in demand-forecasting techniques that are used to set prices and to determine whether reservation requests should be accepted.

In addition to the aforementioned jobs, there may be a variety of support staff in accounts payable, accounts receivable, and collections, again depending on the scope of the operation. In this chapter, we will not have room to explore the work of all of these individuals, but rather we will focus on a few key players. Let's start with the controller.

Taking Control

If a hotel or motel is going to succeed, there had better be a strong hand at the helm of its financial sector. That strong hand generally belongs to the controller. Controllers need to be thoroughly knowledgeable not just about finances but about every other aspect of the hotels or motels that employ them. It is not an ivory tower position where attention is paid *only* to financial matters. Let's hear from those in the field who hold this position.

As the controller for a resort in Squaw Valley, I control the purse strings. I work hand in hand with the general manager, and I count every bean that goes in and out of this place. That means I have to have a real sense of what happens in each and every department of this resort. I have to know if the lounge manager is spending too much, if housekeeping is going overboard on toilet paper, if the activities director has purchased too many beach balls. That's the job.

✨ Sure, you have to be comfortable with figures— that's a given—but you also have to be comfortable with people. It always comes as something of a surprise when I say that, because for some reason, I guess the general reputation regarding those of us who are in the accounting field is that we're not usually the life of the party. That may be true, but then again that doesn't mean we don't have to be good with people. Anyone in a managerial position—and a controller is first and foremost a manager—has to be good with people. You have to be able to make sure that people are doing their jobs without making them feel uptight or defensive or inadequate. The role of a manager is to motivate people to do their best.

✨ As the controller, I'm a kind of cop—both a traffic cop who makes sure that things go smoothly, and a law enforcement official who checks to see that things are being done right. I have to monitor each department in the hotel to determine whether the money is getting to the bank as it's supposed to. I have to check to see that sufficient revenues are being generated to pay the vendors and the staff. This is not a job that you can coast along in.

✨ In this line of work, you have to be very detail oriented. For example, let's say you've got a group that's holding a banquet and you've extended 30 days' credit to them. Now that's all well and good—but has anyone actually checked their references? If not—and if you get stuck—that's going to blast your profit margin big time. So you've got to be constantly vigilant, because when money mistakes are made, that becomes a very serious business.

🔱 My staff and I generate an enormous amount of paperwork. We deliver daily reports to the general manager and the executive committee, assessing what's happening on the sales, labor, and purchasing fronts. How do the actual figures compare to the budget? How do they stand up against projections? How do they look compared to last year's figures? These are the kinds of questions we ask *every day of the year.*

🔱 I'm not just a number cruncher, although I certainly would never take offense at being called that. After all, crunching numbers *is* at the heart of what I do. But I'm also an advisor. I'm continually involved in helping others in my hotel understand how they can improve their operation *from the vantage point of profit and loss.* If I'm sitting in on a food and beverage meeting, let's say, and they start talking about how they'd like to put in a wood-fired oven because the hotel across the street has one, I have to ask the crucial question: How are you going to pay for that? Have you figured out how many pizzas you have to sell to justify your expenditure? People outside of accounting don't always ask themselves these kinds of questions.

🔱 Just because you're the top man on the totem pole doesn't mean that you don't have to roll up your sleeves and get to work and do the numbers along with everyone else. The controller can have a staff of a dozen bookkeepers and auditors and what have you, but there comes a time—many a time—when she's right there in the trenches putting in her time.

🦋 I think a big part of a controller's job, which often won't even get a mention, is the fact that you need to be out there educating people. You know, 10 years ago, most people knew nothing about computers, and now we realize that we all need to know at least something about them, so that we don't have to bring in the technicians every time some little problem comes up. I think the same principle applies to accounting. I don't see why every person who works in the hotel shouldn't have some basic grasp of elementary accounting principles. In fact, in the last year, I've even introduced a series of lunch hour workshops on accounting principles, and I've kind of strong-armed certain people to come by and learn something. They have, and you know what? They're darned glad they did.

🦋 Whenever a new manager comes on board, I ask to sit down with that person and I explain everything I think that person should know about the income statement for his or her department. I haven't encountered anyone so far who's objected to my little tutorial.

🦋 I'm the controller for a hotel in Acapulco, and I take the mentoring aspect of my work quite seriously. I see a lot of talented people coming in to fill managerial positions in our hotel, and I always say to myself, "José, you can help those people realize their potential." I'll invite them down to the café, and we'll have a coffee and we'll just talk. I'll hear their ambitions and their plans, and I'll bring a financial perspective to all of it. Gently . . . always gently. I'll invite them to consider a financial angle they may not have thought of. These people may be terrific—creative and industrious and dedicated and full of energy—but they can be even better when they start incorporating financial thinking into their worldview.

🔔 Don't forget the aspect of managing your own department. That means developing staff that knows what it's doing and making sure that your department is neat and orderly and inspires confidence in all those who come into contact with it. Of course, that should be true of any department in the hotel, but somehow mess and money make for a particularly unfortunate combination.

🔔 When you're talking about the financial area, I cannot overstate the importance of ethics. Okay, now you're going to tell me that ethics is important in every area of the hospitality industry and in life in general, and I couldn't agree with you more. It's absolutely unethical for a culinary professional not to wash his hands after using the bathroom. But in accounting, ethics is really center stage, because there is such temptation around money. Just read the paper these days, and you'll see what happens when ethical lapses occur.

Dollars and Sense

Given the space limitations of this chapter, we will not delve into the specific functions of the accounting staff. Between the general cashier, the paymaster, and the various auditors and personnel in accounts payable and accounts receivable, there are just too many players to describe in detail. Instead, we have polled these individuals about general information and principles that must be understood by people entering the financial sector of a hotel's or motel's operation. The following points were made:

🌽 First things first—never confuse *finance* with *accounting.* They're two different things. Finance means managing your company's monetary resources and income. Accounting, on the other hand, is the tool used for finance. Balance sheets, income statements—these are accounting tools that are used in the interest of finance.

🌽 Accounting is an absolutely beautiful science. You've got your resources (i.e., your *assets*), and you've got the claims against your resources, which are, of course, your *liabilities.* Your job is to make the assets come out on top.

🌽 If you reconcile your checkbook, then you're involved in a simple accounting system. You're keeping track of your payments, your receipts, and your balances. If you *enjoy* reconciling your checkbook, then you might actually have a future in finance.

🌽 Let's start with square one. If you're in business, you're looking for a profit. Are you with me? The idea is to increase the value of the investment. How do you do this? By taking in more than you pay out. Accounting methodology is designed to help you make sure that you're doing just that.

🦀 It's important to point out that one of the functions of accounting is to create reports and other materials that are of use to investors, creditors, and people *outside* of the organization. These reports do not have to be as detailed as the reports for managers and others *inside* the organization.

🦀 In a very real way, accounting is the same in all businesses and industries. All accounting reports take into "account" business transactions; they process data and information; and they generate results—the proverbial "bottom line." But in a very real way, too, accounting differs from one industry to another. Some businesses will expend a great amount of their resources in marketing, a sporting goods manufacturer, for instance. Others, let's say a biotechnology firm, will spend less on marketing and more on research and development. A construction company will have much of its assets tied up in equipment, while a bank will have a large proportion of its assets in loans and investments. The hotel and motel industry is interesting, because its two main aspects are really quite distinct as businesses: lodging and restaurants. So while there is a sameness to the accounting for both halves, as there would be with any two businesses, there is also a definite difference. That's one of the things that makes this a challenging business to work in.

🦀 I'm an old-timer. I started in this business as a kid, working as a busboy in a restaurant on Cape Cod. Now, decades later, I'm the controller for a resort in Lake Placid, New York. Let me tell you—it's been a long, uphill trip. But I think the biggest change I've lived through is the coming of the computer.

Nothing has impacted more on accounting, nor on the hospitality industry in general. Today, anyone can—and everyone does—use spreadsheets. With a spreadsheet, even someone running a B&B on an island off Maine can think like a big-time controller. You can run your occupancy percentages, your sales volumes, your average checks. You can generate your income statements, your balance sheets, and your budgets. Once you've inputted all your data, then you can experiment.

 Beyond the accounting function carried out by the controller and his staff—that is, the creation of accounting reports like balance sheets and income statements—there's also the financial management of the company. In large companies, like hotel chains, for instance, the person at the top of the heap who is in charge of this financial management will usually be the vice president of finance, or the CFO, chief financial officer. The aspects of financial management that we're talking about here include budgeting and forecasting, cash management, raising capital, tax compliance, and risk management.

Auditing

One of the most important functions of the finance department is auditing. In fact, large organizations may have a seperate internal audit department. The responsibility of this department is to audit—that is,

Quick Facts on Financial Management

To get a sense of what is involved in the financial management of a hotel or motel, you should become familiar with the following concepts:

👑 **Budgeting.** The operating budget allows management to create strategic corporate planning and holds the individual departments to the specific revenue, expense, and income targets stipulated in the operating budget.

👑 **Cash management.** Got some extra cash on hand in one sector of the operation? Is cash badly needed in another sector? Large corporations may count among their personnel a cash management officer who is in charge of moving that cash around. Cash management involves investing surplus cash in marketable securities that provide a return but can also be cashed in quickly as needed.

👑 **Capital funds.** Large hotels are often in need of expansion, just to keep up with the competition. Did the hotel across the street put in a pool? A fitness center? A casino? Whoa! There comes a time when you may need money for this sort of thing, or just a major overhaul of what currently exists, and your cash requirements will exceed your cash flow. At such a time, the CFO may raise funds through things such as public financing (selling common stock or bonds to the public at large), bank loans or credit lines, or financing from insurance or leasing companies in the form of mortgages or other long-term loans.

❧ Tax compliance. It is the job of the finance department to make sure that any and all tax returns required by the government are filed in a timely manner. In a very large organization, there may be a tax department to deal with these matters.

❧ Risk management. The finance department also will see to any corporate insurance needs that will protect the hotel from casualty, property, and liability losses.

systematically check and assess the financial records of an organization or part of an organization—in order to make sure that the various sectors of the corporation are operating as they should be. The internal audit department usually will be headed by the general auditor or the vice president, audit.

Another place you'll find the word "audit" is in the job title "night auditor," a common position in the hotel and motel field. This person confirms the hotel's or motel's accounts every day, updating credits and debits for each room rental and, in hotels, for each department. Let's hear what our night auditors have to say about their work.

❧ Maybe you guessed it—this is a night job. I usually start around 11 P.M. and finish up around seven in the morning. If you've never worked a night job before, it can take some getting used to. You might find yourself looking at the world in a way that's radically different from most people, and that's not for everyone.

👑 True, it can get a little lonely in a night job, but hey—I'm in Las Vegas, so I don't even notice. Plus, in a big hotel like mine, the night auditor has company. In our department, it's me, three other auditors, and a food and beverage auditor. We're one small happy family.

👑 Basically, if you don't understand what we're talking about here, the night auditor balances all of the guest folios against all of the departmental room charges. That way we can make sure that if someone ordered cracked lobster and champagne from room service, it'll appear on his bill.

👑 As a night auditor, in addition to verifying charges, I also post the room rate and tax on each guest's folio, I produce the end-of-day managerial status reports, I prepare the list of arrivals for the next day, and I'm called upon to perform front desk activities as needed. So even though it's legitimate to call me a number cruncher, I've also got quite a bit of pure clerical work involved in my job.

👑 An important part of my work is making sure to check a guest's credit limits. My predecessor let five members of a rock band live like kings for a weekend . . . and then found out that their cards were maxed out. That's how I got my job!

👑 Another part of my daily routine is to look over the records of the housekeeping department. That way

I can make sure that there aren't any sleepers—rooms that don't show up on the computer as available when in fact they are.

✥ Usually it's up to the night auditor to update the city ledger. If you don't know what that is, it's the tally of all the money owed to the hotel after the guests' folios are closed. When a guest checks out, the folio is closed, and if there are other charges, like those billed to a credit card, it goes into the city ledger to be collected when the credit card company pays out. Charges incurred by skippers or walk-outs—guests who've cut out without paying their bills—go into the city ledger, along with disputed bills, bad checks, and all that.

✥ Management and sales get a lot of important raw data from my department. I tell them which of those parties that made reservations actually arrived, how many walk-ins we had, how many no-shows there were, and stuff like that. I give them the number of overstays—people who stayed beyond their planned time—and the number of understays, which, as you can figure out, were people who didn't stay as long as they planned. All of these figures go into the management's projections.

✥ Let me tell you one thing about the night audit: it's a difficult position to fill and to keep filled. Not everyone wants to spend time in a job like this, where sometimes it feels like you're in one world and everybody else is in another. But it's a great way to learn the hotel business. You can move nicely into a management position from being a night auditor . . . and if you're a student, let's say, by day, and can manage to grab 40 winks in the afternoon, it might be an ideal job for you.

🔖 The centerpiece of the night auditor's experience is what's called the "trial balance." That's when we ensure that every report, posting, and transaction that's been collected and audited is accounted for. Most property management systems (PMS) run a trial balance at the end of the shift before the night audit is finalized. That's when things can get a little crazy. You might have hundreds of transactions to go through, and you've got to make it all come out right in the end. It's nerve-wracking at first . . . but then you really kind of get into it.

Property Management Systems

A property management system, or "PMS," is a night auditor's best friend. This computer program performs the lion's share of the auditor's nightly accounting duties. Unfortunately, you can't just push a button and take a long nap. The auditor needs to organize the data. But it's hard to imagine life before the PMS came along.

There are many property management systems on the market from which to choose. The U.S. Government Accountability Office (GAO) has a useful pamphlet on how to assess them. You can download this pamphlet on the Internet by going to the link below:

<http://www.gao.gov> Enter keyword "gao-02-171g" to access the report.

Yield Management

Another interesting area for number crunchers is *yield management*, or *revenue management*, which basically entails making the necessary calculations to maximize the amount of income or revenue to be realized from room sales. Let's hear from the professionals.

I've been in the hotel business for almost 25 years, and I'd say that the rise of yield management is one of the biggest changes in the business overall. The idea of yield management—where you're basically forecasting to see how you can maximize your resources and revenues—isn't new, but the technology behind automated yield management is very new indeed, and very exciting. The automated systems tell you pretty much everything you'd want to know about the hotel's history over the past years (i.e., how well it did this spring as compared to last spring as compared to 10 years ago); which sector of the hotel is doing best (high end or budget, corporate or leisure); and a whole bunch of other things. It's amazing what you can learn today just by pushing some buttons.

As a revenue manager, I spend a lot of time in meetings. I kick off every day with a revenue maximization meeting—we call it the "revmax," for short. It's me, the general manager, the director of rooms, and the entire sales and catering staff. We sit around and look at what happened yesterday. We look at any sales leads that may have come up. We review the rate strategy for the day and for the next few days ahead. Then I'll have a weekly meeting like that, which we call the "revenue management meeting." We go over the numbers in much more detail, examining our rates, any upcoming trends and marketing strategies, and more. So, in other words, to make it in this position, you've got to like meetings, and you've got to know how to run a tight meeting—no easy feat.

Basically, if I had to say what my job was in a nutshell, I would describe the revenue manager as the person responsible for forecasting the number of rooms sold and the rate being paid for them over a particular period of time. I have to be aware of all sorts of factors—not just history, which counts for a lot, but what's going on in the neighborhood. Is there a jazz festival? A marathon race? Anything like that is obviously going to have a big impact on rooms sold. Then I have to be aware of any special promotions that our competitors might be running. And then I have to know what the weather's going to be like. If a hurricane is blowing in, that's going to have a heck of an impact on my forecasting.

Once you've got your forecasting nailed down, then you start reconciling it with your expenses. How much are your labor costs? If you're selling X rooms that week, then you need X housekeepers, right?

Forecasting is the centerpiece of my work. I'd say it takes up about three-quarters of my time. What do I do with the rest? I devote that time to checking out new avenues for revenue growth, I'll run a systems check on revenue channels coming into the hotel, I'll explore aspects of our reservations department, or I'll do liaison between sales and operations—that sort of thing.

🪶 I like to study the demographics of our guests. Who are they? Where do they come from? Why are they coming to Cleveland? Are they here on business or pleasure? How often do they come? So forth and so on.

🪶 An extremely important aspect of my job as revenue manager is making sure that our various revenue channels are all systems go. That means, on a frequent basis, I check our 800 number, our central reservations office, our Internet site, the local convention and visitor's bureau, the global distribution system (GDS), and more. The last is the really important one that all the travel agents use, and you can have a problem and not know about it for months if you aren't vigilant.

Global Distribution System

A global distribution system (GDS) combines airline, car rental, and hotel reservation systems under one umbrella. These are a boon for travel agents, who can do one-touch shopping.

We have only touched on the fundamentals of a handful of positions in the finance sector of the hotel and motel field. Other important areas are purchasing, risk management, and investing, which unfortunately we cannot spend time discussing here. But before we leave this chapter, we'd like to dispense a last bit of advice. As a hotel or motel professional, you will have to crunch numbers at some point or another. Business is, after all, about dollars and cents, bottom lines, budgets, and so on. There is really no area of the hotel and motel field where you won't have to put on a quantitative hat now and then. Now many people suffer from what has been identified as "math phobia." When they look at numbers, they glaze over, and their mouths go dry. This response is entirely unnecessary and like any phobia can be overcome. Let us spend just a few moments exploring this subject.

Overcoming Math Phobia

The fear of math is every bit as real as the fear of spiders, water, heights, or germs. It is a fear that strikes women in particular, who as children may have felt disenfranchised in math classes where boys were the ones most often selected for recognition. As we said earlier, math and business are inextricably intertwined; therefore, it is important for anyone in any kind of business—the hotel and motel field included—to have a certain comfort level with mathematics. Some good tips for conquering math phobia follow:

As with any phobia, avoidance only breeds more intense fear. Confront your fear. Look it in the eye. And don't run away from it.

❧ Do not give in to negative self-talk. Don't tell yourself that you're stupid, you're hopeless, you're a lost cause. No one is, and you're only making the situation worse by beating up on yourself.

❧ Approach mathematics as if it were a foreign language . . . which for you it decidedly is! You wouldn't berate yourself if you didn't know French or Italian or Russian, would you? You'd learn it, at a pace that felt comfortable for you. Many times, we're turned off by math in our early years when "the teacher goes too fast." We may be forced to relearn math as adults, but now we have the motivation, which comes out of need. That helps.

❧ Start modestly. Take a college-level class in book-keeping. You *can* do it. You'll see. And this time, don't be afraid to ask questions and get all the help you need.

❧ Mathematics is not primarily about memorization. It's about using your brain in a way that can open up doors. You can become phobic about math if you feel that you can never get numbers to stick in your head, but when you realize that math is more about theory and less about memorization, the whole idea of mathematics becomes less stressful.

❧ Overcoming your math phobia is like overcoming your fear of technology. A lot of us, in this computer age, felt that we would never be able to master the basics of computer literacy. But most of us have, isn't that so? We've learned how to use e-mail and the Internet and how to create and send files and even do spreadsheets. If we could learn that, then why shouldn't we be able to learn the fundamentals of math as well?

Having devoted this time to the number crunchers, we now move on to our next chapter, where we present some of the jobs that didn't fit into any of the last three chapters. We'll take a look at the positions of executive housekeeper; directors of engineering, marketing, human resources, and sales; and of course general manager.

Chapter 11

All about the . . . Supervisory and Support Staff

If ever there was a case of last but not least, this is it. Although this is the last in our group of chapters about the various jobs in the hotel and motel field, it profiles some of the most important positions, chief among them the general manager. So, let's get down to business, since we have a lot of ground to cover in the pages ahead.

The Buck Stops Here

At the top of the hotel hierarchy sits the general manager, often referred to simply as the "GM." This individual bears the ultimate responsibility for the

243

operation of the hotel. Keep in mind that we are differentiating between the general manager and the chief executive officer of a hotel chain. A hotel chain is a large corporation, and its executives usually sit in a suite of offices far removed from any one hotel. But in this chapter, we are talking about the top person—the mega-manager—in the hotel itself. Of course, the general manager will report to the hotel's owner or owners, but on a practical, day-to-day basis, he or she is "the boss." He or she makes the decisions and has to be everywhere and anywhere, checking to make sure that everything is going as it should. Let's hear from our general managers what the job is really like.

As the GM of a hotel in Branson, Missouri, I would say that the thing I do most is talk. Face-to-face and on the phone, all day long. And when I'm not talking, I'm e-mailing. I have direct, purposeful contact with upwards of 50 to 100 people a day. Most of these contacts don't amount to more than 10 minutes each, but believe me, these exchanges can be very concentrated and very demanding, and they pile up.

To be a GM, you have to be able to tolerate a long day. I understand that president George W. Bush goes to bed every night at nine o'clock and always finds an hour a day for his fitness routine. Me, I rarely get into bed before midnight, and if I have an hour to myself during the day, I don't even know what I did right.

I'm the GM of a hotel in New Orleans, and I decided a long time ago to give up on the idea of having a tightly structured schedule for myself. I go where

I'm needed when I'm needed. In other words, I do a lot of troubleshooting. Half the time I'm just sort of walking around, smelling out problems, if you know what I mean.

🦀 As a female GM of a hotel in Boston for the last four years, I can tell you that being a GM and being a woman do not go together in the eyes of a lot of the people I work with. It's always been considered a real man's job, requiring a great deal of confidence and energy. Now I don't know why I say that's a man's job, because heaven knows women can have confidence and energy, but not everyone really believes that. Of course, now that we've had women like Margaret Thatcher and Indira Gandhi and Golda Meir running countries, you'd think people would realize that women can run hotels. But it's still an uphill struggle, given that.

🦀 While it's true that as a GM I make the final decisions, I'm glad to say that I've been able to put together a really dynamic executive committee that supports me all the way. This includes my rooms manager, the controller, the food and beverage director, my sales and marketing director, my director of engineering, the director of public relations, the director of human resources, and the director of convention services. They're all terrific. Then again, if they weren't, I wouldn't have them on the committee. You've got to be pretty ruthless about stuff like that when you're the GM. That's called "being a leader."

🦀 I've got to tell you—one of the real perks of this job are all the perks. I live totally rent free with my family in a beautiful apartment on the hotel grounds. I pay nothing for our meals. I get an extremely generous entertainment budget. You put all that on top of my salary and other benefits, and you've got one heck of a package.

🦢 One of the most important aspects of my work is interfacing with guests. I learned that lesson from a master. The most profound influence on my professional life was my first boss, the GM of a hotel in Switzerland where I went to work right out of hotel school. He could be a terror with his staff, but with the guests he was as smooth as *schlag* (whipped cream, in case you didn't know). Just the way he did, I talk to the guests, I mingle with them, I make sure that they're happy. If they don't seem happy enough, I troubleshoot with my staff to figure out what we need to do to make them happy. When it comes to guest satisfaction, I count very few failures.

🦢 All my days start out the same. I'm in at 6:30 in the morning. The first thing I do is stop by the front desk to pick up my report from the night audit staff. How many rooms were occupied? What kind of ADR (advance deposit reservations) have we got going? Did any pressing guest issues come up? A question I always ask is if we "walked" anyone. (In case you don't know it yet, to "walk" a guest means to send him or her off to another hotel because you didn't have room.) Then I scope out the daily banquet events, and I check in with the food and beverage people. And that's all before I have my coffee!

One thing I tell people is that you have to allot time in the day for reading the newspapers and checking in with other media sources. As a GM, you need to be tuned into what's going on in the world at large and in the world around you. In other words, you have to stay informed on economic trends and current events that could impact on your business, and you have to know what's going on in your neighborhood. Are there plans to build a toxic waste dump two miles down the road? That would be a good thing to know, wouldn't it? Is there a blockbuster Picasso exhibit opening up at the museum? This is information you'd want to share with your guests. Plus, reading the newspaper gives you all kinds of ideas about sales leads. Let's say there's a story on some big military reunion coming to town in three months. You can send the article down to sales and tell them to get on the case.

I'd say the single most important thing about being a GM is to be a good, effective motivator. A lot of our staff has very hard work to do, and they don't always enjoy that much appreciation. Take housekeeping, for instance. I make it a point to stroke them. We hold special luncheons for them twice a year where we give out awards and prizes. It makes such a difference to them . . . and, ultimately, to us!

Don't forget to network with other GMs in the area. It's very important to stay connected. We don't talk room rates—that's against the Sherman Anti-Trust Act—but we can talk about upcoming conventions and the Chamber of Commerce and what have you.

When it comes to the job of GM, the bottom line is that it's really about the guests. You have to make your guests feel absolutely safe, happy, and satisfied. And to do that, you have to go the extra mile, many times a day. We just had a kid—a six-year-old—visiting us who lost his teddy bear. Everyone in the hotel was out looking for it, and we finally found it at the bottom of the linen chute, hidden among the sheets and pillowcases. Now that was an adventure, but it's all in a day's work for a GM and his or her people.

Director of Operations

In a large hotel, the general manager's person-in-waiting is often the director of operations. What does this person do? Let's hear from the professionals.

As the director of operations for a large hotel in Dallas that services successful business professionals, I'm one of five who sits on the executive committee. It's me, the director of human resources, the director of sales and marketing, the controller, and the general manager. Our guests pay a premium price and expect the best. I make sure they get it.

For the last five years, I've been director of operations for a four-star resort in the Virgin Islands, and the real centerpiece of my day is our operations meeting at nine o'clock every morning. All the department heads show up for it, and we discuss yesterday, today, and tomorrow. It's a little like going into the war room . . . except that we have the chef's award-winning scones to help move things along.

👑 I'm essentially the GM's right-hand woman. One of the things that my GM has delegated to me is the task of team building. (I was on the Olympic equestrian team years ago, so he knows that I know a thing or two about teams.) To that end, I not only have my operations meeting every morning with the entire staff of department heads, but I also routinely meet one-on-one with each department head over the course of the day for 20 minutes to a half hour. I hear their problems, and I help them figure out solutions. And that's how we stay a team instead of just a bunch of people working under the same roof.

👑 For a few years, before I went into the hotel business, I was in construction with my father and my two uncles. Now, as director of operations for a hotel in Atlanta, one of the aspects of my job that I enjoy the most is overseeing and managing capital projects and purchases. A new boiler? A new sidewalk? A sewage pump in need of repair? It's all done through my office. What can I say? I love it. I'm a real "home improvement" kind of guy. And now I oversee about $2 million in renovations a year.

 *Director of Engineering*

The director of engineering is intimately involved with the physical aspects of the hotel's operation. Falling under his or her purview is a staff that might include any or all of the following:

- chief engineer
- carpentry specialist(s)
- electrical specialist(s)
- plumbing specialist(s)
- painter(s)
- interior designer
- landscaper(s)

Today almost all major hotels and resorts also maintain a complete business center, and the business center manager often reports to the director of engineering as well. Being the director of engineering, in other words, is a bit like being a project manager, or the "clerk of the works." Let's hear what it's really like from those who hold this job.

🔱 I'm the director of engineering for a resort in Stowe, Vermont. People come to us for skiing, for the foliage in the fall, for our lakefront activities in the summer. It's a fabulous, all-season showplace that we have here, and I love it. I think loving the place you work for gives people in my line of work a real boost. Having pride of place is so important. I know every little nook and cranny of this resort, and I take care of every need that comes up.

🔱 I'm the beeper guy. I walk around and get calls from everyone. The front desk, the catering staff, the valet—they all want a piece of me. And they all get it.

✨ Obviously it's vital to keep a history of whatever repairs have been made. The last thing we want is for a guest to come back to us and find the same problem he experienced on the first visit . . . because then you can be sure there won't be a third visit!

✨ The executive housekeeper and I are very close. She and her staff are the ones who spot most of the problems in the rooms. Leaky faucets, running toilets, broken shades, rugs that are buckling—the executive housekeeper gets on the horn and lets me know.

✨ Very important: as director of engineering, your job is to keep a schedule of inventory and maintenance. You need to keep track of which machines have to be oiled daily, when belts should be changed, when motors have to be oiled. That's the job.

✨ As the director of engineering for a top hotel in Portland, Oregon, I love to be a guest in other hotels and to walk around and see all the things that aren't done right. I don't know why that gives me so much satisfaction, but it does. I'll walk down the corridors and see rips and tears in the wallpaper, and I'll know that they're there because housekeeping and room service carts didn't have the bumper wheels like they ought to. Then I'll find myself wondering why the director of engineering didn't install base and chair rails. That would have helped a lot and could even have made for a nice design feature. Then I'll look up at the ceiling and I'll see scrapes there too. Doesn't the director of engineering in this place know about orange-peel or spatter-texture paint? It would hide those scrapes beautifully. Then I'll go into my room and I'll see that the blackout curtains have punctures in them that let the light come through. So much for sleeping late in the morning. You could fix those punctures easily with vinyl tape, if you cared. And the bathroom toilet has a leaking flapper. Doesn't the director of engineering realize that you can waste about 6,000 gallons of water a year that way? Okay, you get the point. I can't stop criticizing when I stay at somebody else's hotel. I really feel, however, that you wouldn't be able to say the same if you stayed at my hotel. Why? Because I care.

Executive Housekeeper

The executive housekeeper's job is a very important one in the hotel hierarchy. The executive housekeeper, or the "housekeeping manager," reports to the director of services and supervises a staff that includes the assistant housekeeping manager, the room inspector(s), the housekeepers, and the laundry manager. Some executive housekeepers comment on their work.

I'm very satisfied with my job, except that when I tell people what I do, they sometimes look at me funny and say, "Oh. You clean rooms?" Actually, I don't—not that there's anything wrong with cleaning rooms, thank-you very much. I started my career in the hotel and motel field right out of college in the rooms division of a chain hotel in Columbus, Ohio. Somehow I got fascinated with housekeeping, and that's how I came to be what I am now—executive housekeeper for one of the most exclusive resort hotels on the island of Bermuda. Like anyone in a managerial position, I motivate people to do their best. That's really what my job is about. And my staff is probably the largest of any department in the hotel, with one of the biggest budgets. So it's a big job.

In the housekeeping area, you can never settle for second best. You can't be "sort of clean." You can't have a "medium-clean" bathroom. There is an absolute standard that you do or do not sign onto. In our hotel, I set the bar for housekeeping, and believe me, I set it high.

I'm the executive housekeeper for a 450-room hotel in Little Rock, Arkansas. We're big enough to have a full-service laundry, so that comes under my helm too. That's a whole other job, if you ask me. I'd like to off-property our linens and uniforms, but so far, no.

For the last eight years, I've been the executive housekeeper for a resort on Kauai Island in the state of Hawaii. It's paradise for me, as I grew up in Bismarck, North Dakota, but the job has its share of difficulties. One problem is that some of our housekeepers are ferried over from another island, and if there are weather problems or mechanical problems with the ferry, which has happened, I'm caught shorthanded. Still, I'd rather be shorthanded in paradise than fully staffed back in the Plains states.

One of the very interesting things about being an executive housekeeper is that, almost invariably, you'll be managing a highly diverse staff. I'm at a hotel in Chicago, and my people come from all over. El Salvador, Bosnia, Cameroon, Cambodia, Poland—it's fascinating. And sometimes confusing. I have to do a lot of training with my staff and with other departments in the hotel to deal with language problems, cultural values, and so on.

Your staff is continually involved with difficult physical labor. They're bending over to make beds. They're pushing and pulling heavy weights. They're exposed to germs and bacteria. They're working with equipment that poses risks, like sheet and towel folders and garbage compactors. Part of your job as executive housekeeper is to work closely with your hotel's department of human resources to make sure that you're meeting OSHA requirements, and that no one on your staff is placed in jeopardy.

Remember this: you are the leader of a big team. I have morning meetings where I'm giving marching orders to 70 housekeepers using a bullhorn. To handle crowd scenes like that, you have to learn how to be a good leader. To me, that means recognizing who the informal section leaders are—the ones that the other housekeepers look up to—and getting them to be your allies. You have to learn how to become accessible so that people can complain to you before a problem becomes a Problem. You have to learn which people from which culture don't like to look you in the eye, and you have to learn how to teach them otherwise, while still respecting their cultural precepts. It's a challenge, but like all good challenges, figuring out how to overcome it can be exciting.

Do Not Disturb?

What exactly is meant by the "Do Not Disturb" sign that housekeepers find dangling from the doors of rooms? It means different things in different hotels. Executive housekeepers interpret these three words in the following ways:

👑 We have a policy where our housekeepers call the room before entering. If no one answers, I tell the housekeepers to leave a message and then try entering. A little complicated maybe, but it works better than anything else we've tried.

👑 I've worked in hotels where the rule was that every guest room had to be physically entered at some point within a 24-hour period. In our hotel, I've set the rule to be 12 hours. I'm a lot more comfortable with that.

👑 One of our rules is that we wait two hours after checkout time before we enter the room.

👑 I have my staff leave messages on cards in the room telling the guests when they'll be back the next day.

Whatever the policy is, make sure it's clear to the guests. At the very least, post the policy in the in-room guests' directory.

It's wise to become very knowledgeable about products. Listen to vendors, go on the Internet, network with others in the field to see which cleaners really work without causing toxic damage to those who use them, which uniforms allow the wearer to "breathe," and stuff like that. Don't expect to know everything—nobody does—but do ask the right questions.

You want to know my worst nightmare? Celebrities. Rock celebrities. Don't even ask!

I think it's really important to build an *esprit de corps* among your staff. You know, more than likely, you're going to be dealing with people who come from backgrounds of being oppressed, who haven't been treated all that kindly by life. Don't compound that. Work against it. Let them know in little ways and bigger ways how you value them. Come in some days with a digital camera and take candids and post them on the bulletin board. It's fun for everyone. We're up here in Minneapolis and when spring finally rolls around, I bring in daffodils for everyone. It doesn't cost me much, and I get a lot of goodwill out of my investment. That's the way you have to think in this job, and you know what? I like thinking that way.

Good workers can be hard to find in this area, so you have to sometimes make do with what you have. I have some housekeepers who are fine with the rooms but don't do a great job on the bathrooms. So I put them together with those folks who do bathrooms well, and we have a kind of tag team going. That works out nice.

The Turndown

Some of our executive housekeepers felt that the turndown service—the process by which the hotel room is made warm and inviting, usually conducted between six and nine in the evening—was one of the most important aspects of their department's work. Their comments follow:

🔱 I think it's very significant in creating guest satisfaction. We always do an amenity presentation—a truffle on the pillow, pastel mints—and that's what makes going to a hotel feel different from staying home.

🔱 In our hotel, we close the drapes, we turn on the satellite radios to soothing music, we fold the spread down from the pillows . . . we create an atmosphere.

🔱 This is a good time too for tidying. We empty ashtrays and wastebaskets, pick up clothes from the floor, dispose of any obviously used linens, fluff pillows, and so on.

🔱 As the executive housekeeper, I'm also in charge of maintaining the lost-and-found department. You wouldn't believe what turns up in there! Musical instruments, dentures, eyeglasses (well, I guess you *would* believe eyeglasses). It's really something else. I maintain a system where I log in each item with the date

Loss Prevention and Security

Protecting hotel guests is of paramount importance. This matter is attended to by the security staff, headed by the director of loss prevention, whose job is to ensure that all accidents, thefts, and other such problems are handled professionally and thoroughly. A large hotel of 1,000 units may employ a security staff of 16 persons or more, as well as a number of off-duty police officers who work on an hourly basis. These security personnel do not wear uniforms, and only the off-duty police officers can make arrests. Any and all of the security personnel can, however, use handcuffs, when called for, as in breaking up a disorderly scene. Security also is routinely involved in patrolling for prostitution-related activities.

found, the room number or area it was found in, a description of the article and its condition, the name of the person who found it, where I've stored it precisely, and when it's claimed and who claimed it. That pretty much covers all bases.

 ## The Selling Game

When you come down to it, there's really no more important function in the operation of a hotel or motel—or any retail business—than selling your product or service. Selling of hotel and motel rooms and services is handled by the marketing department, which is headed by the director of marketing. Among his or her associates are the following:

- director of group sales
- sales manager(s)
- director of transient sales
- reservations manager
- transient sales manager
- reservation agents
- administrative assistants

In our chapter on the front office, we briefly discussed reservations, which often are handled these days away from the actual hotel site. In this chapter, we focus on the nature of hotel or motel sales in general.

Specific responsibilities of the marketing department include selling hotel or motel rooms and facilities to guests and groups of guests, supervising all advertising, managing public relations, to keep the hotel in the public eye, and fostering relationships with travel agents and tour guides. In large chains, these functions usually are dealt with in the corporate offices.

Principles of Selling

Whether you are the director of marketing, whose job entails researching trends and making major tactical decisions, or the sales manager, who is primarily responsible for selling rooms, the principles of selling remain the same. A crash course from our sales experts follows:

First and foremost—know your product or service inside out. You can't sell something that you don't know thoroughly.

✦ Enjoy people and smile. Make eye contact. That is so important. Leave the sunglasses at home, even if you're walking around in Arizona in midday showing a prospective customer your property.

✦ Crossing your arms, crossing your legs, fidgeting— these are all no-nos for sales personnel. They signify disinterest and/or defensiveness, which really are anti-thetical to selling. On the other hand, if you're with a customer who is crossing his legs, you could try doing the same. That's called "modeling," and it's an effective way to get somebody to come around to your way of thinking. After all, imitation is the highest form of flattery.

✦ Learn not to interrupt. The public has a negative image of the fast-talking snake-oil salesman—you don't want to be like that. Nobody enjoys being interrupted, and as a salesperson, you don't want to go anywhere near something that nobody enjoys.

✦ Beware of barriers. Let's say you're at a trade show, sitting behind a table, expecting prospects to come over and sit down across from you. Instead of that, try placing the table against the wall so that you can work from in front of the table to eliminate the barrier. Same thing goes for your office. Don't sit behind a desk. Arrange a few chairs so you can be close to your prospect. Same thing goes for a conference table. If you're dealing with a group, quickly identify who seems to be the lead decision maker and sit next to that person at the table. Proximity helps sales enormously.

Telephone Selling

Poor telephone technique can ruin sales more quickly than just about anything. Remember the following golden rules on telephone sales:

👑 First of all, answer it! If a phone rings more than four times without being answered, you've lost that sale. Answer it on the second ring at most.

👑 Make sure the person hears your greeting. Don't rush it or garble it.

👑 Whatever you do, force yourself to sound interested . . . without sounding like you're forcing yourself. You might be having the worst day in the world—your goldfish died, your car's making a funny noise, you've got a sinus headache, you can't find your favorite mug—but that's not your customer's problem. You have to sound as if you're having a really great day. So do it!

👑 Don't put anyone on hold. If you do, you've lost the sale.

Marketing

How does a hotel or resort get its name out there? That is a problem the marketing department must solve. Advertising is expensive, particularly television advertising, so it should only be used selectively, if at all. We asked our directors of marketing which other kinds of strategies they use. Their answers follow:

👑 Dedicated toll-free numbers are invaluable, and they've become much more affordable. Nowadays, telecommunications companies typically provide a detailed call report with the billing. Basically, what you do is you assign a dedicated phone number to each of your primary marketing vehicles, so that you've got one 800 number in your newspaper advertising, one on your corporate Web site, one in your public relations efforts, and when your bill comes in, your staff can review it and issue a usage report letting you know how most of your customers are finding out about you.

👑 I like business reply cards inserted in magazines or attached to brochures. These are highly efficient measurement tools.

👑 Coupons are a good way to keep track of your restaurant advertising. They make nice gifts too.

👑 I think the best tool in the marketing toolshed is your reservations agent. Tell the agent to take a few seconds every time she or he books a guest to ask how the guest found out about your hotel.

👑 In terms of public relations, the rule I was always taught is that a well-placed story is worth three times as much as an ad. And a good public relations firm can always find a news angle. Just make sure you engage a PR firm that has strong experience in the hotel field with good contacts and multimedia and techno savvy. It's not enough today for a PR firm to only know newspaper and magazine editors. They have to have contacts in broadcasting, the computer industry, and promotions organizations.

Ongoing Training

Sales is a tough business. The director of marketing and the general manager should promote the ongoing training of sales personnel. There's always a better way to sell. Keeping it fresh is part of the challenge. Let's hear how our GMs and directors of marketing handle this issue.

👑 As the general manager of a hotel in Kansas City, I drop in on the marketing department for five minutes early every day. I do a "go team!" number. If I notice that someone is looking very tired and wan, I'll pull that person aside and determine whether there's a real problem going on. Maybe she's got a 24-hour bug and should be at home. When people are under the weather, they shouldn't try to be out there selling. It won't happen.

👑 I'm the director of marketing for a resort in Alberta, Canada, and one of the things that I first learned when I was a youngster in sales is that a really good director of marketing will make a point of being with his or her staff a lot. That means going out on calls with staff members or sitting in on meetings with prospects or joining in on a dinner or lunch that a sales-person is having with a prospect. It's called "observing," and then giving feedback. So important!

👑 Of course, you have to review a salesperson's weekly sales activity. That means sitting side by side and looking at what worked and what didn't. Super-vision is the name of the game.

👑 I find it a truly amazing thing that some of the managers I know don't do much with motivation. Sales is all about motivation—motivating a prospect to do what you want him or her to do. So how can you not motivate your staff? I have prizes, awards, employees of the week and month . . . the whole nine yards. And I'm always thinking about new and fresh ways to motivate my people.

👑 Positive reinforcement for good work is the rule and gentle suggestions for alternatives when the work is not so good. It's never, "You screwed up here, Max." It's always, "Let's look at this, Max, and see how we could have done this differently."

Human Resources

One other executive-level position in the hotel and motel field that we'd like to discuss briefly is the director of human resources. This individual is responsible for hiring or screening potential personnel and training them. In a business where labor needs are high and where there is often a rapid turnover of employees, the HR director is a key player on the team.

The human resources department has the following duties:

- recruitment
- payroll
- benefits

- orientation and training
- conflict resolution

It's a fascinating area, as testified to by some of the HR directors to whom we spoke. Their comments follow:

👑 Just managing a payroll when you've got maybe 1,000 employees is a heck of a job. Nothing disgruntles people more than a late or incorrect paycheck. We make sure, to the best of our ability, that it doesn't happen.

👑 This can become a very complex job when you think about all the OSHA regulations and whatnot that you have to stay on top of. Not to mention all the nuances of benefits packages. You need to be a very thorough and detail-oriented person for this line of work.

👑 You have to like people. When you're interviewing, you can't sit there like King or Queen Tut. People are nervous; people need jobs. You have to really care about people if you're going to be encountering them in these kinds of situations.

👑 I network constantly with others who hold this position in other hotels. There's always interesting new stuff happening with training and new things you have to know about OSHA and so forth, and that's a great way to stay on top of the curve.

👑 Know that you're going to deal with some really tough issues when you're in this job. Stuff like sexual harassment, age discrimination, substance abuse, workers with disabilities. These things will come up, and there are no nice simple, easy ways to deal with them.

Conducting an Interview

The centerpiece to hiring a job candidate is the interview. Our HR directors offer the following suggestions for effective interviewing:

👑 Ask open-ended questions that really get a candidate to open up and talk. That's how you get to know someone.

👑 Be careful not to ask any questions that could be interpreted as discriminatory—age, marital status, nationality, religion, stuff like that.

👑 I write out all my questions and check them off—discreetly—as I go along. I want to make sure I don't miss anything.

👑 You're going to want to ask skill-based questions—What does a candidate know? What can he or she claim mastery of?—along with behavior-based questions, like what he or she would do in such-and-such a situation.

👑 Allow silence. Some people need time to formulate their replies. There is nothing wrong with a thoughtful person who takes the time to do that.

👑 Ask each candidate the same questions. That way you won't get into an apples-and-oranges situation when you're weighing their comparative merits.

You have to understand that part of your job is protecting yourself and your hotel against charges of negligent hiring (failure to uncover a job applicant's incompetence or lack of fitness before hiring); negligent retention (failure to be aware of unfitness for a particular job or to take corrective action, such as retraining, reassignment, or discharge); and negligent entrustment (giving a job to an unfit employee that places another person in danger). These are all very serious charges that carry huge liabilities, and if something goes wrong, you're the one who's going to catch some of the heat. You can count on it.

This chapter concludes our look at the most significant jobs in the hotel and motel field. In our next, and last, chapter, we discuss how to get hired for these jobs.

Chapter 12

The Savvy Professional

L et's call a spade a spade: looking for a job is hard work. It requires time and organizational skills, and for most people, it almost inevitably involves some degree of disappointment and frustration. Few people immediately get the job that they're hoping for. Most have the experience, at least some of the time, of interviewing for a job that they really want and suffering the letdown of not getting it. When this happens more than a few times—and it is perfectly normal and to be expected for it to happen more than a few times—a crisis of confidence can occur. This is particularly true for young people, who may not yet have hides that have been toughened against what they perceive as rejection. To ward off negative feelings that can cloud the job search process, it is helpful to have a good understanding of what the process is all about. That way you can guard against personalizing the normal, if unpleasant, things that can happen in the course of such an activity. This chapter offers a good start on giving you that understanding.

You also should be encouraged to know that the hotel and motel industry has a high turnover, thus job opportunities often are plentiful. Of course, in a difficult economy, people travel less, both for pleasure and business, and the lodging field can suffer. But with our national economy showing signs of renewed health, you should be able to proceed with your job hunt with a sense of cautious optimism. The important thing is for you to do your absolute best with the part of the process that you can control. Try not to lose sleep over what you can't control. Life's too short for that.

As a general rule, success comes to those who work at it. One way to work at success is to manage your career smartly. You need to be flexible, *pro*active instead of *re*active, and always looking toward the future. If you're in a job that no longer feels right—let's say the standards of the hotel or motel are not up to *your* standards, or if you feel that you are being exposed to unethical behavior, or your employers have not figured out ways to show their appreciation for all of your hard work, or you're just feeling burned out and dead-ended—then it's time to do something about it. Doing nothing is counter to success.

A good place to begin our discussion for those seeking a job in this field is the concept of professionalism. It is important to know that you will be judged on your professional attributes, such as your attitude and your actual record of attendance at work. That means that you have to show up for work on time every day and have to prove that you know what it means to be a team player. These are ways for you to develop references, which will be very important in your future employment. If you develop a reputation for professionalism, and if you know your way around a hotel or motel, then you should be in a good position when job hunting.

Laying the Groundwork

Even before you start looking for a job—and this is true whether it's your first, second, third, or fourteenth job—you should always do a self-check to assess your current qualifications. Ed Koch, the former mayor of New York City, used to be famous for asking everyone he encountered the same question: "How'm I doin'?" It wouldn't hurt for you to get into the habit of asking yourself that question regularly and often. How *are* you doing? Are you getting to work on time? Are you staying late to do extra? Are you bringing your accomplishments to the attention of people who matter? Are you hearing and accepting critical feedback, and are you acting on ways to improve your performance?

Let's hear how others in the field lay the groundwork when job hunting.

✴ Twice a year, whether I'm job hunting or not, I'll give myself a "report card" with grades. Punctuality? (I'm running a B there.) Teamwork? (B again.) Appearance? (A—my husband says I'm actually too concerned about appearance.) Efficiency? Speed? Reliability? I keep a list of attributes, and I assign myself a grade. And, believe me, I'm a hard grader.

✴ Going out on a job search requires some real planning and preparation. It can feel at times like climbing up a very high mountain, and you wouldn't want to try that until you got yourself into some kind of decent shape, would you? You'd actually go into some serious training. And that's what I do when I start a job search. I go to bed early, so I'm more rested. I lay off junk foods so that I feel better and have more usable energy. I start canvassing close friends and family on how they see my strengths and my weaknesses. While some of what they say might smart a little, I accept it all as constructive criticism, and I act on it. There have been times when I haven't felt as accepting of criticism, and I felt the need to go to a counselor for help with what turned out to be deep-seated self-image problems. Helping yourself in that way—utilizing the input of a professional who is trained in these matters—can be another important step in laying the groundwork.

✴ I look in the mirror—literally and symbolically. Literally speaking, I give myself a good hard once-over. Is my skin clean and healthy? Is my hair smartly styled? Are my clothes neat and pressed? Symbolically speaking, I look into the mirror at the whole me, conducting a honest and an unflinching review of myself. What do I bring to the table? What are my greatest strengths? What areas do I need to work on? I don't just sit there, waiting to find out how I'm seen by others. Instead, I "see" myself, even if I don't always like what I see.

👑 Before you head out into the job market, you have to sit yourself down and be as clear as possible about what your needs and wishes are. Is security at the top of your list? Are you one of those people who are easily bored and feel that you need the fast track and a high level of excitement and stimulation in order to be satisfied? Are you a self-starter, or do you need to be part of a team? Do you have family or school responsibilities that require flexible hours? Where do you want to be in a year? Two years? Five years? Be clear about your passions and your priorities. It makes the job-hunting process so much more focused and productive.

👑 As the human resources director for a resort in San Diego, I'm always hearing about "dream jobs." Well, guess what, ladies and gentlemen—there's no such thing! Dream jobs are like dream families—do you know anyone who has one? Every job comes with its own set of problems, some worse than others. These problems are typically things like too much work, crazy people, long commutes, no room for advancement, or any and all of the above. It's up to you to figure out which of these problems you can live with and which you can't.

When It's Over, It's Over

Leaving a job is a reality of life. Sometimes you're asked to leave—a harsh reality, but it's happened to most of us, and it is to be expected in a shaky economy where companies are often restructuring. Other times you are the one to call it quits. Let's hear how people in the field deal with these job-altering situations.

Termination

There's no way to make getting fired feel good. But it doesn't have to be a Shakespearean tragedy either.

🔱 Not only can it happen to anyone, but it has happened to most people, at one point or another. Remember one thing: you don't always get a good reason for why this terrible thing is happening to you. Sometimes it's something unspoken, like the fact that your new superior hates the way your nose looks. He may tell you it's "restructuring" or whatever, but it's really the nose, and there's nothing you can do about it.

🔱 The first time I got fired, I was completely unprepared. I thought I was the world's best employee. Getting fired never even entered my mind. Then I was caught totally unprepared and had to run around getting my résumé together and all that. Now I live like a CIA agent who keeps a bag packed at all times. I keep my résumé up to date, have my files backed up—I'm ready to go!

✤ Don't fly into a rage when the news comes. This is not the time to spit in your boss' eye or tell him that he looks like Humpty Dumpty. Behave with some dignity. Behaving otherwise will come back to haunt you. You'll go down in legend as the person who went haywire, and that could even inhibit your getting another job, particularly if the professional world you're working in is a close-knit one. If you can leave on reasonably good terms, you can even hit up the boss who fired you for a reference. He might feel guilty enough to give you one.

✤ Feel free to ask for reasons why you're being fired. You're entitled to know. Being laid off because of restructuring or poor company performance feels different—and, I have to say, better—than being fired because people think you're no good at the job.

✤ Check into everything your company might have to offer you in this situation. Of course, finalizing a severance package is the first priority, but there may also be employment counseling, crisis intervention, and other benefits that you can take advantage of.

✤ Don't feel that you have to go around the entire office saying good-bye to everyone. Let a few close coworkers take you out for a drink, and limit it to that. You don't want to go through the whole story with everyone. It's taxing to you and to others.

Instead of thinking of this event as the end of something, think of it as the beginning. That may feel artificial at first, but artificiality isn't necessarily bad. What you have to do right now is play a little trick on your brain. Tell yourself that this is exactly what you needed. You were getting stale and complacent. You needed a change in your life. This could be the start of something big.

Calling It Quits

Being in the position where you're the one who's chosen to leave rather than being asked to leave is certainly a far more desirable scenario, but it too requires some real finesse to do it right. Advice from your fellow professionals follows:

My #1 piece of advice, which I'm sure you've heard from your mother, your father, your aunt, and your uncle, is never leave a job until you *have* a job. Even if you're miserably unhappy, try to tough it out, because you run the risk of being even less happy if you wind up unemployed for an extended period of time.

Even if you've had a history of blowouts with your boss, it's a very good idea, when you finally leave for your new position, to make a nice, clean, friendly break. Don't say the things you always wanted to say. Write them down in a notebook instead, and stick the book in a drawer. If you're the one who has to be the bigger person, then just bite the bullet and do it.

🔔 Never give less than two weeks' notice, no matter how bad things are. Your goal is to come across as a class act, and bad habits, like leaving without sufficient notice, can become an unwanted part of your "résumé" that follows you around wherever you go. By the same token, never give more than four weeks' notice. Even if the situation is basically amicable, too much notice can leave you feeling strained and awkward.

🔔 If you tell your employer that you're leaving, and he or she makes you a counter-offer, give it some serious thought. Why, in fact, *are* you leaving? If it's about the money, might it not make more sense for you to stay than to transition into a new position? If it's about just wanting a change, do you think you might want to stay in the job if some changes were made?

Résumés

Your most important tool when you're looking for a job is your résumé. This written summary of your education and work experience will offer potential employers a quick window into who you are. Some thoughts follow from professionals who work in human resources:

🔔 Unless you happen to also be a Nobel Prize-winning physicist, keep your résumé to one page in length. In the hotel field, there is a lot of turnover, and individuals may have held quite a few jobs in not so long a period of time, so the one-page rule can be tough, but it's probably doable. Just check your résumé for any padding. Is it really important for a prospective employer to know that your hobby is dog grooming, for instance?

👑 Neatness counts, in everything you do in life. Make sure that your résumé is scrupulously neat and clean, with no smudges or coffee stains or any kind of marks on it. Put your résumé on special-quality résumé paper (this is a heavier stock that you can purchase in stationery stores). Don't go rainbow crazy. Maybe *you* think pink is your color, or that orange is cheerful, but other people might hate pink or orange, so why risk it? Stick with white, buff, or gray. To you, that might be boring, but to others, it's classic.

👑 I'm the human resources director for a hotel in the Canal Zone, and do you want to know the thing that really drives me insane? When I get a résumé that looks like someone's put some effort into it, but it doesn't have the necessary contact information. I'm talking about the street address, phone number, and e-mail address. And please make sure that your contact information appears on your cover letter as well.

👑 When it comes to résumés, there's more than one way to arrange them. Some people choose to arrange the résumé by listing their positions in chronological order. Others prefer to arrange it according to their accomplishments or abilities. Check on résumé format with a librarian or on the Internet, and then decide what you're most comfortable with.

❦ Watch out for the "I" word. Résumés should be written objectively—not from a first person point of view.

❦ Keep your language simple and to the point. I know people who whip out the thesaurus and start using over-the-top verbs like *maximized, optimized,* and yada yada. It just looks like so much hot air.

❦ Honors and awards are always nice. Don't forget to list any that you've received (but *not* the 4-H Club blue ribbon for Best Pie that you won when you were 11).

❦ Are your career goals popping out sufficiently? If, for instance, you're aiming to move up into a position as assistant controller, is that clear on your résumé?

❦ If the line of work you're pursuing represents a career change, try your best to convey the transferable skills you'll be bringing with you to this new career. For instance, if you were a manager at a phone company in the past, pitch your managerial skills as part of your current package. After all, a big part of a hotel professional's job usually involves managing people.

❦ Always stress "action verbs." Think in terms of language like *developed, achieved, created, coordinated, maintained, formulated, introduced,* and so on. These are words that make you sound like a powerful force to be reckoned with.

❦ As a human resources person, I can tell you that many candidates lose the chance to even be interviewed for a job because of mistakes on their résumés.

Misspellings and poor grammar suggest that you don't attend to details very well. That means points off, and in this competitive job market, who can afford to lose points on something like that? Ask a friend, a teacher, a family member, or, if necessary, a professional résumé service to give your résumé the once-over to make sure it is error-free.

✥ *Nothing, nothing, nothing* goes into the résumé about salary requirements. Could that be any clearer? Any talk about salary is restricted to your interview, and only if and when the interviewer brings the subject up.

✥ No photos, please. They'll make your résumé look like a "Most Wanted" notice in the post office.

✥ Don't bother to include personal references on your résumé. It's safe to say that almost everyone has someone who can speak well of him or her.

✥ If nothing else, remember this: *never, ever* lie on your résumé. If you do, and the grapevine gets hold of what you've done, then you might have *really* serious problems finding a job.

Sample Résumé Our idea of an effective résumé follows. Of course, other kinds of formats also would be acceptable. Explore which format works best for you by consulting a résumé-writing service, your school, or knowledgeable individuals, or by looking for more information in career books or on-line. (The information below is taken from a real résumé but has been altered to protect the person's privacy.)

Carmen Padilla

853 Madison Street   860-229-3132
West Haven, CT 06516   padillac@hotmail.com

Objective: Hotel Sales Manager

PROFESSIONAL SKILLS
Proficient in computers, including Leisureshopper, Microsoft
Word, Excel, System One, and Apollo.

EXPERIENCE
Travel Agent   1994–Present
AAA NORTHWAY, New Haven, CT

- Provides exceptional customer service and bookings for air
  and train travel, cruises, packages, car rentals, and hotels.
- Maintains up-to-date information on various locations and
  attends regular customer service classes.

Administrative Assistant, Conferences   1993–1994
Services
PITNEY BOWES, Stamford, CT

- Competitively selected as one of two interns to participate
  in the working experience at Pitney Bowes. Responsibilities
  included greeting and registering all visitors to Conference
  Center (98,000 annually), scheduling conference room
  facilities, identifying and coordinating support services
  (audio/visual), assuring appropriate room arrangements as
  needed, coordinating and planning menus with clients and
  Canteen Food Service.
- Assisted visitors in arranging transportation, lodging, and
  communications. Experienced in multiline telephones,
  e-mail, and scheduling through computer.

Walt Disney World College Program,   1993
Merchandise Hostess
WALT DISNEY WORLD COMPANY, Lake Buena Vista, FL

- Nationally selected from over 200 colleges and universities to be a participant in the living, working, and learning experience of the Walt Disney World College Program.
- Responsibilities included maintaining Disney standards in all aspects of job performance in order to provide quality service for over 100,000 guests from all over the world, as well as management responsibilities, philosophy, financial structures, corporate culture, employee etiquette, and protocol for "The Disney Success Formula."
- Lived with international students in a multicultural environment.

Bank Teller   1990–1992
FLEET BANK, New Haven, CT

- Promoted to assistant head teller.
- Provided customer service and monitored multicash transactions utilizing computerized banking system.

Waitress (Seasonal)   1993
WEST HAVEN MUNICIPAL GOLF COURSE, West Haven, CT

EDUCATION
President's List, published in National Dean's List; Ducktorate: a degree from Walt Disney World Company representing outstanding work performance given by the Disney University; selected for internships at Walt Disney World and Pitney Bowes.

A.A.S. Degree, Gateway Community College,   1993
New Haven, CT

CLUBS
Delta Phi Epsilon Sorority

Cover Letters

Everybody talks about résumes, but your cover letter is equally important. In fact, without a good cover letter, a prospective employer may not even be motivated to look at your résumé. Advice from your colleagues follows:

🐾 The most important thing to keep in mind is that your contact information has to be on your cover letter. It's not enough just to have it on your résumé.

🐾 You want to know the worst thing you can possibly do when sending out a cover letter? Using a "universal" salutation, like "Dear Sir or Madam" or "To Whom It May Concern." Every cover letter has to be personalized. If not, you're just wasting the paper you wrote it on.

🐾 If you fancy yourself the creative type, then the cover letter is the place to put some of that creativity, not your résumé. Develop an interesting first sentence. Reference a quote. Do what you will to capture the attention of the person who may be reading your letter. But don't go overboard. Don't write a rap poem or draw a cartoon or whatever.

🐾 Your letter should be personal and appealing, but brief. Don't go into any special circumstances. Don't tell them how you had to sell the family farm in order to go to school. Once you get your foot in the door—no, make that *beyond* the door—then you can get a little more personal.

Sample Cover Letter

Different personal situations obviously dictate different sorts of cover letters. We've chosen what we consider a "model letter" from a recent college graduate in search of a job:

11 Wanamaker Road
King of Prussia, PA 19406
610-214-9976
Todd1498@aol.com

June 28, 2004

Ms. Lillian Ames
The Marriott Corporation
700 Aliceanna Street
Baltimore, MD 21202

Dear Ms. Ames,

I am writing with regard to the position you advertised on www.careerbuilder.com for an Audio/Visual Manager. I graduated this month with my A.A.S. degree in Hotel Management from the Community College of Philadelphia, where I was president of both the Future Business Leaders of America and the American Marketing Association.

As you can see from my attached résumé, I have had extensive experience in the audiovisual field over the years as well, having worked as a sales associate in the electronics department of Best Buy in the King of Prussia Mall for over two years.

Although a recent graduate, I am not a typical new graduate. I attended school in Wyoming, Arizona, and Texas, putting myself through these schools by working at such jobs as bartender, laundry manager, and catering staffperson, all of which enhanced my formal education.

I have the maturity, skills, and abilities to assume a position as Audio/Visual Manager, and I would particularly like to do this in Baltimore, a favorite city of mine where I also have family.

I will follow up this letter with a phone call to see if I can arrange a time to meet with you. Thank you so much for your interest.

Sincerely,

Christopher Todd

🕮 Highlight your skills in your cover letter. If you've gotten special training of any sort, put it right up front in the cover letter. It's a way to grab attention.

 Networking

Above and beyond anything else, the best way to find a job in the hotel and motel field is by networking. As in most industries, the less desirable jobs are usually those that are advertised in the help wanted sections of newspapers. In fact, the U.S. Department of Labor reports that only about 5 percent of job seekers obtain their jobs through the "open" job market, which consists primarily of help wanted ads on the Internet or in print publications. The hotel and motel world is even more of a word-of-mouth industry than most, so networking is key. With your résumé in shape, you can start to target those people you think might be of help. When it comes to networking, keep in mind the following pointers from the professionals:

👑 Once you start networking, you'll be amazed at how many connections you can make right off the bat. There are friends, family members, faculty you've known and all of their contacts, neighbors, merchants at stores where you shop regularly, people in your church or synagogue, or other organizations in which you participate. Start keeping track of them, developing a file or a database, and never look back.

👑 Always carry an up-to-date business card. There is plenty of software on the market to help you make your own, or you can have a few hundred run off inexpensively at any of the big copy centers.

👑 When you exchange cards with someone, take a second to jot down some bit of relevant information about that person on the back of his or her card. Maybe in the course of your conversation you were able to establish that the person was "into" bridge, as you are,

Mingling

Next to public speaking, networking is the #1 fear of a lot of people. Mingling with strangers at cocktail parties is really difficult for many people. Some good networking tips follow:

🦋 The way I learned how to feel comfortable talking to strangers was by practicing it with people outside of my work world. So I'd give myself an assignment. I'd go to my kids' Little League games, and I'd tell myself to strike up a conversation on the bleachers with someone I didn't know. Then I'd find other places where I could practice my skills. The more I did it, the better I got at it.

🦋 If you feel awkward at cocktail parties and other social gatherings, start by approaching someone who *looks* approachable. That's usually a smiling person who makes eye contact.

🦋 If you don't know what to say to initiate a conversation, don't despair. You're not alone. Try something related to the group, the event, the venue, or even the weather. "Don't you just love what they've done to this old hotel?" "Has it ever felt this cold in March?" "Are you as excited as I am about hearing [whoever's speaking that night]?" "Oooh, broiled scallops. My favorite" (if you're standing by the buffet table). Almost any little thing can get a conversation rolling, as long as the other person is up for it.

Business cards follow a conversation, they don't open it. After you've spoken with someone, you might say something like "Do you have a card? May I offer you one of mine?"

One of the hardest things for people is to enter a room where everyone looks like they know each other and are involved in conversation. There's no really neat, cool way to handle this situation . . . just try your best to integrate yourself. What I do is I pick out the noisiest group of three or more people and I stand on the periphery, trying not to look exceedingly odd. I'll smile and sort of nod, giving off body language that I'm available, guys, for conversation, and if there's a halfway friendly person in the group, they may nod back to me, and I'll say something like "You folks seem to be having a good laugh. What's going on?"

Learning to mingle is a skill that, like any other skill, only gets better with practice. Don't get stuck with just one person at a networking event. That's not what it's for. If you need a getaway line, say something like "Will you excuse me? I just spotted an old friend across the room." Then go to the bathroom for a few minutes.

or had a black belt in judo. That kind of information will make for useful "openers" when you try to reconnect.

Keep in mind that networking doesn't just happen at business functions. The whole point of networking is that there are all kinds of people out there who can help you. So if your cousin invites you to join her at her insurance firm's holiday party, take your business card with you.

🔱 If someone helps you in the course of networking—whether it's an actual job lead or just some good information—show your appreciation. We're not talking about a basket of fruit here. Simply drop the person an e-mail to say thanks. That's all it takes.

🔱 Every now and then your networking will lead you up against a stone wall. Some people are just like that—not very friendly. Don't take it personally. Just move on to the next person.

🔱 Don't abuse these connections. If a person is open to networking with you, don't suddenly act like the two of you are the best of friends. That will turn off the other person very quickly. And if a person offers you 15 minutes, limit yourself to that. Don't wait to be asked to leave!

🔱 Help others as much as you can. I'm of the belief that when you help other people, your good deeds come back to help you.

🔱 If you're still in school, take advantage of the guest speakers who come to lecture. Target them after their presentation—but nicely, please—and ask if you could send them your résumé. Many will be open to such a proposition.

🔱 You want to know the real reason why networking works better than almost anything else when it comes to getting a job? Because it's based on real human nature. People aren't helping you because of the goodness of their hearts. People are helping you because they figure that, down the line, maybe you'll help them or their sons or daughters or nieces or nephews. And if you're smart, you will.

👑 Try volunteering with different organizations so you can get your name out there in the community of hotel and motel professionals. If you check into it, you'll probably find that there are fund-raisers scheduled in your area that you can help out at. These functions are a great way to get your foot in the door and make yourself noticed. If people see that you've got the right attitude and that you know how to be a team player, they'll be happy to help you.

👑 Once you start, don't ever stop networking. It's a state of mind. It's not like you reach a certain plateau in your career and then you don't have to do it anymore. You have to think of your career as a work in progress and networking as an ongoing activity that's positive and constructive.

The All-Important Interview

The résumé and the networking are designed to get your foot in the door. Okay, so now that you've got that foot in the door, what's your next step? Your colleagues offer their comments.

When you go for your interview, make sure, first and foremost, that you have identification with you. That means a Social Security number, a driver's license, the names and addresses of former employers, and the name and phone number of the nearest relative not living with you. Don't leave home without these!

First impressions count for a lot. That's just the way of the world. Think of how you've felt on those occasions when a blind date comes to your door. Well, when you go into an interview, you're the blind date. That means your grooming has to be impeccable. Clean, pressed clothes, polished shoes, clean fingernails . . . the whole bit.

A lot of people these days really *hate* perfume and regard it as a major invasion of their space. So leave it off for your interview.

Bring an extra copy of your résumé with you to the interview. Even though you may have sent one beforehand, it can't hurt to have another one with you.

There's no being late for interviews . . . *ever!* You should figure that if you're just one minute late, or even 30 seconds, you've lost that job. Scout out the location of your interview a day in advance. Even if it's an hour away, make the run. It's worthwhile, because if you get lost on the day of your interview, even if you show up officially on time, you may still wind up looking all hassled and stressed, and that won't help anything.

🐱 Smile. Nothing telegraphs accessibility and ease with people better than a smile.

🐱 Be an active listener. Face the other person squarely, with good eye contact, adopt a friendly and approachable posture—no crossed arms, please. Lean slightly toward the other person.

🐱 Matching and mirroring is a useful communication strategy to use in the job interview. You match the other person's mannerisms, and you mirror, or reflect back to him or her, those mannerisms with your own body language. It makes the job interviewer feel comfortable and even respected, which won't hurt your cause any.

🐱 Hey, people—don't treat the interview like a coffee break, okay? You don't walk in with a cup of java or a can of soda or a bag of popcorn. You don't chew gum on an interview. And smoking? Are we kidding?

🐱 Sit up straight and speak clearly, just like your mother told you to.

🐱 Don't rest your bag or any other items on the interviewer's desk. Some people are very territorial, and this will turn them off.

🐱 Whatever you do, do not criticize a former employer. It will only reflect poorly on you.

Anticipate questions. Obviously you know that certain ones are going to be coming up. *Why do you want to work here? What do you think you could contribute to our operation? How would you handle a disorderly guest?* You need to do your homework and make sure that you've got some good responses ready.

Good Questions to Ask

At some point in the interview, you'll be asked if *you* have any questions. This is not a time to be silent. Some good questions to ask when it's *your* turn follow:

Is this a new position?

How many people have held this position in the last two years?

Who would be my supervisor?

Who will I supervise?

What is this company's culture? Formal? Relaxed? Rigid? Flexible?

What do you see as the most challenging aspects of this job?

Are there opportunities for advancement in this company?

May I ask what attracted you to this company?

A wonderful way to generate your questions—and to ensure that you stand out from the pack of interviewees—is to research the company with whom you're interviewing before your interview. If you're going to the Marriott, for instance, find out what's new and exciting about the company. Then, when it's your turn to ask a question, you might say something really informed, such as, "I understand that Marriott is going to expand into [whatever]? How do you think that will change the face of the company?" Some useful Web sites to help you with this research follow:

American City Business Journals. A collection of articles in business publications throughout the United States. <http://www.bizjournals.com>

Annual Report Gallery. The largest collection of annual reports on the Internet. <http://www.reportgallery.com>

CNN Money. The news site with reports on all kinds of fascinating financial happenings. <http://www.money.cnn.com>

❧ Role-playing your interview with friends or family can be very useful. Just make sure you're doing it with someone who knows how to take the charade seriously.

❧ Keep in mind that there are certain questions that an interviewer does not have the right to ask, and that you do not have to answer. Anything having to do with

Sample Thank-You Letter

Lucky Christopher Todd! He did get an interview with Ms. Lillian Ames after applying for that job of Audio/Visual Manager. The thank-you letter he sent her follows:

11 Wanamaker Road
King of Prussia, PA 19406
610-214-9976
Todd1498@aol.com

July 14, 2004

Ms. Lillian Ames
The Marriott Corporation
700 Aliceanna Street
Baltimore, MD 21202

Dear Ms. Ames,

Thank-you so much for meeting with me on July 12 to discuss the position of Audio/Visual Manager that you have available. I appreciated the opportunity to learn more about the Marriott Baltimore and to discuss how my qualifications can meet your needs.

I would like the opportunity to become part of your team. I feel strongly that I can be a real asset to your operation. I believe that my record of reliability and leadership in other positions and at school prove the worth of my candidacy. I look forward to hearing from you regarding your decision.

Thank-you for your time and consideration.

Sincerely,

Christopher Todd

your race, religion, national origin or citizenship, age, marital status, sexual preference, disabilities, physical traits . . . these are all strictly off-limits. If one of these questions comes up, you should politely but firmly state that you do not think the question is relevant to the position being filled, and that you would like to focus on those qualities and attributes that are relevant. The message should sink in, and your interviewer may actually wind up being impressed with your presence of mind.

 It is certainly appropriate, at the end of the interview, for you to thank the interviewer and to ask when you might expect to hear something. In fact, I wouldn't leave an interview without asking that question.

 Don't forget to follow up your interview with a thank-you note. It's required. And it will give you the opportunity to restate your eagerness to fill the position, which could wind up being a key factor if the interviewer is choosing between two or three people.

Salary Negotiations

For some people, talking about money is like a trip to the dentist: they'll do anything to avoid it. But negotiating your salary is a natural part of the hiring process, so you must become comfortable with it so you can do it successfully. Some salary negotiating tips from professionals follow:

 Do your homework. Know what the going rate is for the position being filled. The more information

you have, the more powerful your negotiating position will be.

🔱 Negotiating for a job is not like negotiating for a car. After you buy the car, you'll probably never see the seller again. But with job negotiations, if the hiring goes through, you'll be living with the person you've been negotiating with, so it's important to operate out of goodwill. Keep in mind that if you're being offered the position, that means that the employer you're negotiating with has made up his or her mind that you're the one for the job, and so you both have the same goal: to make this happen.

🔱 There are a lot of "extras" that factor into a total compensation package, and you need to be aware of what they are. It could be vacation time, health insurance, or whatever. Look into all of these, and weigh them carefully when you're making your deal.

🔱 Never lie. If you've got a job history, never say you made more on your last job than you actually did. On the other hand, you don't have to show all your cards. In a way, salary negotiations are a little like a game of poker . . . a bit of bluffing may come into play. Maybe your first time doing it, it won't go as well as you hoped. But with practice, you may wind up winning a few hands.

🔱 Bargaining is expected, but there comes a time when you run the risk of overkill. When you feel the offer is in the zone, then back off. Don't hold out for every last penny. Even if your demands are met, your employer may walk away from the experience feeling that he or she has hired a prima donna. Remember that negotiation is about give-and-take all around.

The hotel and motel industry is full of exciting job possibilities at every level. Keep your eyes and ears open, be proactive about your career, continually educate yourself to develop more expertise, and go for it!

Chapter Reference

U.S. Department of Labor data accessed June 2004 at <http://www.bls.gov>

Index